Mind Your Mind

Shed concealed burdens holding the
mind hostage.

Axel Ienna

DEDICATION

To Carl Jung, without whom,
this book wouldn't have come to life,

to my beloved mum, without whom,
I wouldn't have come to life,

and to my *ego*,
because of and despite which,
this book has come to life.

CONTENTS

ACKNOWLEDGEMENTS

Thank you, ADHD, for making me write a concise book and address my own short attention span.

Warm thanks to all participating patients who allowed me to share some of their stories.

Special thanks to Daniel Öberg, whose artwork was used for this book's cover.

My gratitude to thinkers who inspired me over the years; Eckhart Tolle, Epictetus, Gabor Maté, Michel Onfray, Sam Harris, Yuval Harari and of course, Carl Jung, master of the unconscious mind who opened the door of psychotherapy to millions and blessed us with both mind, and life altering wisdom and quotes.

DISCLAIMER:
As self-help can turn into self-harm in the hands of reckless profit-driven gurus, I urge you to vet this book with the same scrutiny and critical thinking as if I were one and never to not treat it as a gateway to the self-help community.

'*Until you make the unconscious conscious,
it will direct your life
and you will call it fate.*'

Carl Jung

'*I am an atheist, thank God.*'

Ernest Renand

1. INTRODUCTION

Empowering a few hundreds people stuck in the unconscious recreation of the dynamic of their first wound and achieve key breakthroughs, led to this book. It aims to facilitate self-discovery, not by chasing the *who am I* -lost cause- but by shedding the *who I am not* and reclaiming *some* control over two major life hacking forces, running freely in the background without our consent. One is messianic high-tech, with its potent algorithms saturating our attention (*A.I* and soon *A.R* and *V.R*), the other is the unconscious mind, running our *life show* behind our back while rolling it before our eyes. If fate is, then is it set in stone or is it a by-product of the mind? Bit of both? Do stories we tell ourselves alter its course? Reading these lines, flying to the moon, boiling an egg, nothing we do, goes unvetted by the restless mind and especially by its *unconscious* master. Not even our sleep is spared. This formidably influential force shapes the causality of our discomfort into false beliefs and thus root no less than our sense of identity. The good news is that it can be decoded and rewired.

Put differently, hard-wired inherited genetic behaviour can't be changed, but our adaptive behaviour can. Three main forces drive the mind; determinism, randomness and mental self-fulfilling prophecies. I focused on the latter -i.e. Buddha's '*what we think we become*' posture on causality- as it is the only force over which we can reclaim any control. But first things first; a rudimentary distinction between subconscious and unconscious is to think of the former as stored information that can be retrieved consciously and of the latter as information that is not accessible consciously.

Regressive hypnosis creates an in-between, altered state of consciousness enabling to reconnect to the unconscious and thus to the inner self/inner child. That is the space where one can shed old beliefs keeping the adult mind hostage. By debunking myths holding us back, we can then brain-cleanse and detach from dysfunctionalities bugging our headspace and any spiritual potential. And I don't mean to infer to religion, I mean spiritual.

To raise my case, I must contextualise the individual mind within the collective unconscious. Over half of the world population, has turned into instant gratification hi-tech junkies, with millions, watching other people living their lives on social media instead of living their own. As we're clearly headed towards a transhumanistic era (making us superhuman but stripping out much of our humanity as we know it) we could face a digital life, of home confinement, wired up to VR/AR sets, morphing into compliant zombies artificially kept in a state of bliss and denial. Twitter rage -and Twitter itself probably- will be a thing of the past.

We are all born multi-talented but lured away from our potentials, not just by hypnotic high-tech but also by peer pressure and tribal conventions that make the majority cave into standardisation. This *settling for less to fit in'* culture begets unfulfillment, numbed at will with consumerist binging, in a world where narcissism, voyeurism, exhibitionism, short-termism and cancel culture are now cheered and amplified. So, to cope...we cope. It is against this backdrop that I seek to portray the perverse impact of beliefs, preconceived ideas, myths and tales, over our sense of self and identity. The larger part of the book purposely deals with the *'issue'* rather than solutions, since the *ego's* default setting is to deny the existence of emotionally sensitive issues, particularly when, it is it! I therefore spare no effort uncovering the nature of the tricky ego, through various prisms, which is why organised religion is a regular reference, as I couldn't find, in good faith (pun intended), more explicit illustrations of self-identification to circumstantial beliefs. I also call attention to the dangerous identification shaped by the adult mind around emotional discomfort experienced during childhood. To that effect, I expose how the mind's unconscious '*evil twin*' constantly plots '*for our own good*' behind our backs and how one can transition from concealed perverse thought patterns into healthier conscious intentions. To access our unconscious *guided regression* is key; think of a powerful meditation to travel back in time to unearth myths we forged as children and hold us back as adults. By becoming aware of our mind ('*minding your mind*') we get a shot at adjusting a life trajectory, often deviated from its course, needlessly challenging and endured, instead of lived and enjoyed. Once processed by the mind, everything becomes a story. So, I wish for this this book's story to morph into its most beneficial version inside yours.

An African proverb, shining in its simplicity captures the core of guided regression: '*If you don't know where you are going, look where you came from*'.

2. FAIRY TALE CULTURE

We'd be a lot happier if only we could stop chasing happiness. I don't believe we give enough credit to the perverse nature impacting modern culture and society's collective subconscious of the legacy of celebrated authors like the Grimm Brothers (*Sleeping Beauty*) and Charles Perrault (*Cinderella*) who were later brought to the silver screen by Walt Disney and followed by a plethora of animation studios.

Who isn't familiar with tales of a young maid in distress to be miraculously crowned, an indolent comatose bimbo waiting to be rescued by her prince while a psychotic ice queen rants to herself in front of a mirror, from the heights of an ivory tower? Besides storytelling, tales usually carry a moralist tone, such as the triumph of inner-beauty and substance over appearance, as evangelised in *The Beauty and the Beast*. They also portray idyllic outcomes between characters most of whom, in real life, would be diagnosed with disorders such as bipolar syndrome, perverse narcissism or co-dependency, to name but a few. As little girls and boys, we are shown distorted realities around which we forge unachievable expectations leading to a range of misunderstandings leading to disappointment and often resentment. I imagine most adults would at least frown if they were told that innocent stories they were exposed to as kids, set them up for disappointment, even failure later in life and impact critical decisions. Yet, they do. Happiness is a transient high, not a default state. Hunting for it is unnatural, an addiction that will turn one into an addict chasing their next , or original hit.

The mind starts building associations, transfers and projections at infant stage; the reason why advertisers are so keen to capture our attention and weave their brand story into our unconscious, as early on as possible. Thus, young women spoon-fed with happy ending tales like *Cinderella*, unknowingly embark on a mission to meet their charming prince (incarnated as *'Mr Right'*, *'the One'*). Nowadays empowered with *YouTube* and *Instagram*, self-proclaimed female lifestyle gurus improvise and dispense *priceless* relationship tips, diet tips and make-up tips, shared profusely across digital screens by thousands of trigger-happy followers in search of answers and validation.

During these spiritually bankrupt times, about half of the world population struggles to make ends meet or survive, while more than a third spend precious resources in self-serving cocoons, chasing conceptual happiness, crystallised as living like the rich and famous; our modern version of the fairy tale. Wealth doesn't buy happiness, but it does buy everything else, making life a lot easier. It also creates a wide range of brand-new stress and problems that money alone can't handle (and has accidentally created). Material aspirations are pretty much doomed to disappoint and fuel an endless compulsive rush for compensatory ephemeral *'happy'* instants sourced through frivolous consumer goods, smartphone *apps* and *'likes'* on so-called 'social' media. Such low-grade instant gratification is swiftly replaced by states of sub-standard depression, giving rise to an urge for the next hit that will briefly tamper and offset the emotional void and shortage of substance endured. Meanwhile, in real life, princes marry attractive women who earn their seat on the throne by doing…just that; sitting pretty. Besides the *World Cup* (another aspirational platform of identification but predominantly for males) global media seldom rallies as extensively as when covering royal weddings. Lavish ceremonies parading a radiant Kate Middleton tying the knot to Prince William, the statuesque former Olympic swimmer Charlene Wittstock becoming Princess of Monaco (who reportedly ran away on the eve of the wedding and was brought back to her senses with a cool *five-million-euro* cheque, but to hell with my cynicism …). Two generations before, their predecessors, the iconic Diana Spencer and Grace Kelly also incarnated a dream come true, elevated to 'legend' status. As is often the case, drama greatly helps build legends, and both princesses perishing in tragic car crashes certainly fuelled the myth. These sombre outcomes aside, these lucky few women accessing the throne leave behind legions of aspiring females watching in awe someone else reaching their inner little girl's coronation dream.

Why does this matter? Because we're all casualties of an emotional con. Even the prince and the princess, but mostly everyone else. Beyond the glitz of it all, these royal weddings can affect the self-esteem of anyone benchmarking their personal circumstances against events which they know to be out of reach. Such latent self-inflicted brainwashing fosters a sense of missing out and ultimately unprocessed resentment. While liberal meritocracy advocates are repulsed by what they view as voyeuristic privilege porn, envious ladies indulge in remotely worshipping a world they can only project into. Far from being limited to royal families, the fairy tale *celeb* culture, now amplified and weaponised by social media, has proliferated like wildfire and infiltrated our homes, every smartphone and every mind. Men project onto wealthier male celebrities, believing that mimicking such and such an athlete or movie star might be a steppingstone onto the social status ladder. Meanwhile, women source marital wisdom from, housewives' TV shows, lifestyle mags, social media and even the local clergy man for additional unfit advice, from men with the least experience of women...What could go wrong?

Men and women striving to follow the rich and famous in their footsteps, aspire to gain respect from the majority and permanent financial stability. This is happening, despite overwhelming evidence that celebrities are among the least stable and often least moral individuals. Their marital tragedies, breakups and regular rehab check-ins are routinely portrayed in the gossip press as temporary adjustments instead of the pathological behavioural disorders they should be reported as. The subliminal perception that celebs live amazing lives that should be aspired to and imitated persists. In real life, celebrities, despair trying to figure who their real friends are, dealing with one betrayal after another from an envious entourage, feeling entitled to pursue a self-serving agenda at their expense. But thankfully for the media industry, the aspiring wannabe crowd doesn't care one bit. The main opportunity cost I see, for this 'wannabe thinking' must be the net waste of energy diverted from self-esteem building activities to project instead, onto what it must be like to *live the dream* of others. Hardcore fans feel 'close' to their favourite celebs to the point of obsession, as if they 'knew' them (*'fan'* is short for fanatic after all). Just as children do with their favourite fictional characters, fans can project themselves onto a figure who represents their aspirations and who feels familiar to the point of dissociating from reality and tragically, from their own personality. While there is beauty in staying connected to the lightness of our *inner child*, fanaticism on the other hand can be a slippery slope often reflecting emotional immaturity and mental imbalance. This focus on missed opportunities and passively witnessing the success of others at the expense of realising our own potential, litters the graveyard of so-called *failures* with fateful *'could've'*, *'would've'* and *'should've'* corpses. Progressively, and rather monstrously, the unconscious mind, weaves these into the fabric of our psyche and self-perception of who we think we are, *deep down*.

As waste of brain power goes, flicking through a gossip magazine ranks high. The scientifically crafted illustrated stories designed for us to check out from daily dullness and look forward to the next one work a charm. After all, publishers are entitled to expect a return on their behavioural consumer psychodynamics investment. What's more, gossip media *'readers'* often form their relationship insights from those. Men won't figure *'what to do with women'* in men's lifestyle mags, but perhaps from women's magazines instead; at least they offer clues about how women think. Meanwhile, women won't find out much that they don't already know about men, by reading either women's or men's magazines. I reckon that fasting from gossip media would go a long way to simplify relationships, as might, pondering over the following generalisation: by and large, men are the doer type, welcoming directives: not being yapped at, but being told what needs to be done, with sufficient background. On the other hand, most women seem to crave authentic attention: being heard, listened to, their views and feelings being acknowledged. Speaking of, let me draw your focus onto the power of acknowledging, which is easy to deliver and brings instant gratification to both parties. I am talking about getting slightly out of our way to hold the door for someone, give way to another driver, halt a bus for someone running towards it or simply say hello to a stranger, an elderly standing by their window; these little gestures go a long way, both to the giver and the recipient. I have lost count of people who admitted to not feeling any gratification from sending money to charity but feel disproportionally good when trading niceties with strangers after they held a lift open for them in a hotel lobby. Experiencing the humanity of a situation leads to favour instant and concrete gratification over deferred, abstract gratification. Now, onto the ubiquity of the *mind conditioning spectrum* and why falling for it is inevitable unless one lives under a rock. While living like the rich and famous is a life aspiration for millions, there are plenty of other compensatory anchorage platforms within and around which one can forge an artificial sense of belonging and of identity. Platforms that one wouldn't necessarily think of as such, because of how deeply engrained (native for some) they are within the psyche. Getting some perspective feels especially meaningful at a time of generalised loss of identify, mass standardisation and constant mind numbing via devices that ironically, create the illusion of splendid personalisation and individuality and of enhanced control. The ultimate '*trojan horse*' invasion of the mind has happened in plain sight. And we seem to love it as much as we resent it.

It matters to call a spade a spade and take a closer look through the lens of *brainwashing*, which is what intensive repetitive mind stimulation is. As French philosopher La Boétie observed in *Discourse on Voluntary Servitude*: '*control can only exist on a consenting crowd*'.

Most phenomena and communities wouldn't survive without the capitulation of rational thinking, essential for brainwashing, indoctrination, and self-indoctrination to take root and develop. Common ingredients to that recipe for (spiritual) disaster are the need for a leader, a hero, thinkers who can think instead of us, coupled with a strong desire to relate, a quest for validation and for status among peers.

3.BRAINWASHED TO BELONG

Conditioned for Tribalism

Our communities couldn't flourish without our acceptance of representations (money, institutions etc) and our natural bias towards tribalism. Such bias is built around two cognitive primal needs: the need to *conceptualise the self* by anchoring to clearly identifiable representations and their labels: '*my job, my neighbourhood, my clubs, who I vote for, pray to* etc...And the need to narrow down the number of individuals we should feel safe connecting with. To that effect we use an *adjustable lens* through which we zoom in and out of our default '*tunnel viewing*' and the mind can model things, places and people. For example, sports supporters will usually resent at least one other team in the league they follow. But when a player of that unloved team is selected to play for the national team at an international game, they will cheer for that player, in the name of a greater cause (the nation), shifting the focus of their antipathy towards a new, albeit temporary, common enemy (in this case; another country). Since the usual sworn enemy is now fighting for your interest and national (read 'personal') identity, it's okay to temporarily move the goalpost. Especially if the player in question who you usually enjoy booing scores for your country. Then for a while, this player, represents you till the game is over, so you can zoom out and revert to bashing him for the rest of the season. Thus, our tribe feels grounding and identarian but is really an ephemeral moving target only subsisting in the mind because we grant it meaning. Tribalism is both a prodigy of division and of unification that concomitantly has us fighting in herds or preventing division and chaos.

Let's take a tour of familiar community types and phenomena through the lens of the brainwashing they rely on to exist. Also, to gain perspective while doing so, imagine how you would explain these (attending a game, religious gathering etc...) to friendly aliens having come to Earth in peace, to understand our habits and our rituals.

Fashion, Sports and Entertainment

Fashion is often embedded into clan culture, as seen in sports and music but also gangs, organised religions and special interest groups (such as *Harley Davidson* bikers for instance). While the fashion industry itself is creative, *fashionistas* are often among the most conformist individuals you'll ever meet. Adapt your clothing style to your environment and your salient personality trait is conformism. I have seen with my own eyes people becoming hipsters just to fit in, grow a beard, wear braces, and painfully push on that vintage bike in tight trousers. The religious term *'icon'* isn't routinely used in fashion (and the celebrity scene) by accident; top performers capture the imagination of the public to the extent of being iconised into living divinities in the eyes of their adoring fans. By the by, neither is the term *'fashion victim'* used innocently. Oscar de la Renta, the designer who allegedly coined the term, (later endorsed by Giorgio Armani) had no shortage of sarcasm with labelling his customers. Fashion's superpower is to make laymen and laywomen feel prettier, taller, smarter, wealthier by simply projecting into an idealised figure through the act of wearing a prop endorsed by the icon they worship.

In sports, beyond the fashion accessories and the chanting while junk food binging, the obvious and most extreme form of tribalism is the *hooligan* phenomenon, the use of violence to express loyalty to a team. Sport is the last thing at stake for those gruesome formations and has everything to do with compensation, the need to fill a large emotional void in a failing psychological structure, vulnerable to mental illnesses and often, cross addictions. It is also common to observe among non-violent supporters, a disproportionate emotional attachment to their local team, particularly if they have been going to the stadium since childhood. It isn't unusual for fans to show up at work miserable, even struggling to cope if their team lost over the weekend. Such a seemingly strange disproportionate reaction breaks way below the surface of a game not meeting expectations; it taps into a bruised sense of identity and the ego hurting. If you are uninvolved in sports and you hear that *Real Madrid*, the *Lakers* or the *Patriots* lost a game, your mind rightfully registers this information as; *a team has lost a game* (and another has won it). But if you are a committed supporter, the simplified version of what the mind experiences goes along those lines, '*My team lost. It sucks. Winning is a sign of strength, losing a sign of weakness. I am my team. My team lost. I am weak. I am a loser*'. And vice versa if your team has won. It is even more devastating, when your team loses a derby to the local sworn enemy or to a lower ranked team. The detached way -dear to *stoicism*- to observe this happening is: '*I attended an event showcasing a flock of millionaires in blue jerseys I support, lose to another flock of millionaires in yellow jerseys. As a result, despite being born with an organic supercomputer in between my ears, I feel like a loser, craving sugar and fatty food to cope*'. Sport isn't simply great to watch, it is also great to practice, engage in, play and discuss. But it shouldn't be a factor of influence into the formation of our sense of self. Imagine if we identified with opera singers we like and go see perform. Why don't we? Or why not identify with real life unsung heroes who save lives for a living? What if sports teams were only awarded points for acts of sportsmanship and the beauty of the game? Some near misses account for the finest gestures ever recorded in sports and are forgotten. Why not, instead of rewarding yet another fake dive from players who shamelessly trade off their morality for a chance to score, we awarded points to clean tackles and players voluntarily signalling fouls they just committed? We don't, because doing the right thing sounds good but looks dull. It also doesn't reflect enough of what we're like, and since we need to relate to our team, we need players to be more like us. We need to admire something greater than us, but we also look out for familiar flaws, trickery, and treachery that we are capable of. Think no further why our politicians are elected on grounds other than their integrity, honesty, or dedication to justice.

Politics

Concomitantly losing steam and becoming more polarised globally, politics still represents one of the sacred cows of the self-identification pyramid. Badmouthing how someone eats, talks or the way they look might cause offence, but you'll get away with it. But don't dare criticise anything about their local team, their faith or trash who they voted for. We *accept criticism about what we haven't chosen*, what feels out of our control or things we judge as unimportant. But if our ego dictated a decision to pick, follow or endorse something or someone, it consequently led the self to identify with it (*my* president, *my* team, *my God*). The ego will therefore fiercely defend that position to dodge risking the unbearable void of a crumbling sense of identity. Even if our vote for a president was passionless and disillusioned, once our vote goes in, the psyche anchors to whatever horse we bet on. If someone is disrespectful towards *our* president, we feel entitled to react to what the mind processes as a personal offense. Below the surface, it is the ego which is being threatened and stimulates the urge to preserve our sense of self. Although as a matter of fact, that person we voted for, the team we go cheer every other week, and the *God* we worship have nothing to do with us. Nothing whatsoever. They only wield power that we grant them over our sense of self. This self-identification phenomenon has been flawlessly legitimised by the mass adoption of millions for centuries.

Gangs and Mafias

Gang culture is still hot and raging. If you haven't been brought up near or in a gang it's easy to wonder why, anyone in their right mind wouldn't just leave the *hood* and start over somewhere safer. The reality is that, if gang life is all you know, it has shaped your mind and your identity to levels that feel like a point of no return has been crossed and your fate has been sealed. What you wear, how you speak and deal with your daily fears by scaring (and scarring) others, has been shaped by the *hood*. Survival is eating up any energy you could deploy to focus to set off onto a brighter life. The only future you can project into is gang life, and death. No matter how dysfunctional, leaving means becoming invisible. Few are prepared to take such leap of faith that demand no knife, no gun but a new mind set.

Mafias also bear a profound stigma of branding and identification that are hard to part with (besides the additional risk of being hunted down and killed if you do). The notion of *foster family* in mafias is just as prevalent as it is within gangs; beyond a lifestyle and easy money in return for high risks, you are given the family that you feel you never had, or indeed, that you actually never had. It is no wonder that criminal organisations, just like cults, attract lost youngsters from dysfunctional families or orphans. The pathological need for a sense of unity enables the emotionally deprived orphan to wilfully self-indoctrinate, and often produce the most loyal members of the organisation they join.

Cults, Religions and Spiritual Fellowships
That old chestnut: would religious believers have turned believers anyway had they not been born in a religious family? And of that same faith? Some believers grow out of their native faith into atheism or into a different faith, but most don't, and some atheists chose a faith later in life, but most don't. These two marginal subgroups belong to two parent groups which are; individuals born into a faith and remain in it for life and faithless individuals who remain faithless for life. Our immediate environment undoubtedly shapes our beliefs, especially during the early, formative years of our lives.

For clarity's sake it is fair to differentiate cults - as they are commonly understood- from organised religions by acknowledging that most religions are not dangerous whilst most cults usually are. In fact, no religion is dangerous but for its ideological or political misuse throughout history. However, modern cults mirror religious foundations in the sense that they defer to a leader (prophet) the one embodies a higher power (*God*) but typically run profit making agendas at the expense of the psychologically vulnerable. The dim *Scientology* movement -made up by a quirky prolific Sci-Fi writer- is now an official religion, ruthlessly conning its members for money and their servitude. As French philosopher Michel Onfray puts it; '*a religion is a cult that made it*'.

The overlap between spiritual fellowships and cults is just as evident as the one between cults and religions. *Landmark* is known as a hugely profitable cult preying on the vulnerable, while the nebulous, multi-dimensional *Masons* bear the traits of a lobby with tentacles stretching from humanities to politics. Like *Scientology* adorning the *religion* label instead of that of a cult, *Landmark* is usurping its affiliation and should be called a cult and not a spiritual fellowship. On the other hand, addiction fellowships (*AA*, *ACA*, *CA*, *CoDa*, *NA*, *SLA*, *AlAnon*) are driven by good intentions beyond doubt and don't ask for money. However, they request equally dire brainwashing requiring a life of daily repetitive rituals for fellows who attain (physiological and emotional) sobriety to remain in the ranks of recovery. The main difference between a cult and a spiritual fellowship is the role of time and money. If you are gradually being encouraged to commit unreasonable amount of your time and money to help the cause in exchange for spiritual rewards, you have been enrolled in a cult that you had better quit for your sake and that of your family. Beyond financial contributions, these structures rely on a deep level of self-indoctrination without which these sandcastles would crumble, and members vanish to start therapy to deal with the aftershock.

Contemporary Art

If you want to test your tolerance levels, take yourself to a respected contemporary art gallery, showcasing multiple artists (to get a fair sample), randomly pick any piece and ask for its price tag. Then try to wrap your mind around the fact that someone out there will pay the ridiculous asking price you were given. Repeat the experience at will with other pieces on display to eliminate any doubt that the oversized, inflatable toilet seat you picked and enquired about was accidentally priced for six figures. Of course, I am oversimplifying and there are great pieces of contemporary art that you and I could grasp, if we were initiated to the artist's creative process and the underlying narrative supporting the product: I mean; the *work of art*. Be that as it may, beyond its apparent absurdity, this niche market obeys a sharp commercial logic based on rampant manipulative speculation and a truly dire form of brainwashing. A dear friend and owner of contemporary art galleries in Paris and LA summed it all up: '*Contemporary art is ruled by gays and Jews.* I often *I wake up wishing I was born Jewish instead of gay. I could always have turned gay, but I can't become Jewish.*' Tell that to the blissfully unaware collector feverishly explaining to his in-laws, over an otherwise enjoyable Sunday roast, why he spent a year's salary for a piece of deformed plastic that should quintuple in value once it wins the highly coveted *Turner* prize. The originally hedonist and noble hobby of art collecting offers a telling example of elitist manipulation by a nebulous cartel brainwashing the uneducated to invest in '*pump and dump*' schemes. Returns seen during the peak of the Internet stock market bubble pale in comparison to the stratospheric returns enjoyed by savvy in-the-know investors and the lucky artist who become a *tier one* speculative household name. Ask Jeff Koons, whose small size iron *'Rabbit'* (arguably the biggest waste of iron since the *Titanic*) just sold for a cool ninety-one million dollars.

Family, Marriage and Parenting

I realised that the holiest of all *'sacred cows of brainwashing'* might be the institution of marriage and family. A native anchorage woven into the fabric of our subconscious by a unique umbilical bond, having all popped out of our mother's womb. Therefore, how dare I bring brainwashing into the miracle of life itself and subsequent family living? Despite recent waves of progressive disruption, societies are by and large still running on the patriarchal archetype software, whereby men are largely defined by their profession and social status while women are graded on their homemaking, housewife track record. Conversely, these two paradigms might be profoundly challenged by transhumanism in the future, as science fiction is increasingly becoming science. Call me party pooper but imagine, a global job market reduced to a fraction of its current size by A.I coupled with robotics, and the rise of bioengineering where *'augmented'* cyborg children would outsmart their parents in a way that would emasculate and strip them of their sense of identity and 'raison d'être'. The transition towards *augmented humans* bears a huge and rather horrific risk of accidental dehumanisation and of a psychological aggression, so profoundly transformative that its ramifications can neither be grasped nor even conceptualised yet. Regardless of such dystopian perspective, the western world has seen a breakdown in marriages with global divorce rate approaching fifty per cent, led by countries such as the UK, the USA, Germany and France (at fifty five percent) and -surprisingly given its historical Catholic tradition- Spain at a staggering sixty five percent divorce rate, explained by a combination of divorce only being legalised in 1981 and the financial crisis ripping the country apart in 2007. Measured by religion, Hinduism has by the far the lowest divorce rate of only *one percent*, followed by Islam at a distant twenty percent. When factoring in the culture of arranged marriages and divorce being a taboo, capital sin in Hinduism, the correlation of higher peer pressure and dogma with lower divorce rate becomes crystal clear. Beyond the numbers let's consider the emotional wreckage caused by the so-called reconstituted families where the prior '*de-constitution*' leaves children in states of fear, fuelled by logistical, emotional, and mental imbalance. Let's also not underestimate that while not having children comes with the certainty of missing out on guaranteed amazement and personal epiphanies, it also comes with the absence of anxiety, stress, disappointment, displeasure and of course, the projection of our own flaws and fears onto a child who didn't ask to be here in the first place. Also, shouldn't the combination of our destructive impact over the climate coupled with bio scientists working tirelessly to extend life expectancy by decades and millions of abandoned kids populating orphanages, make one pause to consider filing for adoption instead of procreating? Is nature's call to reproduce and our sense of entitlement to do that impossible to resist? Perhaps our wiser *alien visiting friend* would beg to differ. It's because I thought really hard about my children, that I chose to not have them. With that in mind, my contention is that the miracle of childbirth can be celebrated but not proclaimed as woman's vital sense of achievement. Today, outside repressive communities, the odds are against lasting marriages, and the trend could accelerate due to a technological revolution challenging the paradigm of the family institution as we know it. Celibacy and a life without children can be a blessing in disguise for some, and for all we know -if the future will be transhumanistic, it is quite likely for marriage to become a thing of the past altogether.

Superstition

Besides being tightly knit into the fabric of religion, other cults and spiritual fellowships, superstitions can be found everywhere. Walking under a ladder is bad luck, so is breaking a mirror - let alone on Friday the thirteenth-, crossing the path of a black cat is a bad omen but finding a rabbit's foot will bring you luck etc... Superstitions mostly bear a negative connotation and find a natural habitat to nestle in, into deeply anchored mentalities such as Judeo-Christian guilt. From a mind conditioning standpoint, superstition is just a latent obsession. Ancient obsessions passed on, surreptitiously or in plain sight, from one generation to the next. Superstition is a conditional prophecy based on the belief that '*If this happens then this will happen*'. Superstition isn't an obsession of the addictive kind like cigarettes or *Instagram*, but rather a latent, reactive obsession connected to fears which can be triggered by an appropriate stimuli (black, cat, ladder, doomed day etc...). It's a cunning form of brainwashing requiring no maintenance to subsist within the unconscious.

Star Wars and *StarTrek* conventions

Besides being great fun to attend, themed conventions fully express the meaning of the word *fanatic*, the attendees, dressed up as the characters they worship embodying what dedication to a cause looks like. Make no mistake, these fans endeavour to think like *Luke Skywalker* or *Mr Spock* when dealing with real-life situations ('*what would they do*') and can't resist an opportunity to show off their best *Captain Kirk* or *Chewbacca* impressions, regardless of the 'social price' they might be paying. Sci-Fi fans offer hardcore examples of identity fusion with made-up characters. Let's not lose sight of how fragile the boundaries between reality and science-fiction have become for some. While *Star Wars* fans have campaigned for years to make *Jedism* an official religion, *Scientology*, which belongs to Sci-Fi as a matter of fact, has developed into a shady, powerful cult of lunatic bullies before becoming an official religion, possibly even more profitable than Christianity (in *revenue per member* terms).

The Case of Synchronicities and Precognition

On the face of it, this topic is trivial but, in my opinion, deserves its own book, which I have in fact, written. We still don't know whether hunches, premonitions, repetitive visions, dreams, and observable patterns are always random, sometimes random, or might follow some intangible mysterious protocol. Synchronicities are for now packed in the 'law of attraction' *new age* suitcase and even if searching for them can turn into an obsession, the mind conditioning is mild and deeply unconscious. You are buying a red *Lexus* and you start seeing red *Lexus* everywhere. You are thinking of getting married and everyone around you is suddenly tying the knot. You are aching to break up and everyone is now filing papers for divorce. How much more of a trend setter can you be? The subconscious, heavily focused on our preoccupations, will hacks our visual and cognitive sorting capabilities to validate our current intentions (that I am buying the right car, should get married, break up etc...). This 'cognitive recalibration' is textbook search for *confirmation bias.* However, some baffling synchronistic events are so far impossible to explain by today's science. I for one, have personally experienced precognitions that are too specific to process as random events.

When you gravitate in spiritual circles you are told that seeing random series of identical numbers, usually in clusters of *threes* or *fours* (but *twos* will do), isn't random and has a symbolic significance, that can be *Googled* and should be contextualised into your personal circumstances. A *222* infers to "being on the right path", *444* that you are "being protected", *777* symbolise inner strength etc... If you start watching out for triple *ones*, triple *twos*, or the clock showing *11:11* you will see more of those so called "mirror numbers". There will be occurrences that will make you swear that they are too spooky to be random. And they probably are. I experienced such improbable events, both unintended episodes and conjured up ones. To put it mildly they felt mind-boggling, unsettling, and wonderful at the same time. But if I am honest, they changed my life in a rather marvellous fashion. As a matter of illustration, I decided to share an episode I experienced that might make you conclude that I am after all, a nutter. The head scratching episode involves a black cat. I am running along a trail in Pennsylvania and spot a black cat, standing still on the side to my left. *Othello*, the magnificent black angora I grew up with immediately comes to mind, as always when I see a black cat. Then, out of nowhere, I am telling myself that *'if we live in a simulation as in the movie The Matrix, then I am going to see another identical black cat right now'*. Just like when in the movie, *Neo* experiences déjà vu with visions of the same black cat twice within seconds. Then, seconds later and less than twenty meters further on the opposite side, I see another, identical black cat, standing on a small hill that was totally outside my vision range when the thought hit my mind. The exact replica of the cat I have just seen. I have run this trail about forty times but never saw any kind of cat before or after that day. From a probabilistic viewpoint, the numerous variables at hand make this occurrence particularly challenging to rationalise; while it is likely or highly likely to see two identical cats at once, it is less likely to see one, then think of seeing its twin and see it. It is even less likely to see it *after* attaching a specific meaning and a condition to it (telling yourself that *if we lived in a simulation then you should see an identical cat* to the one you just saw). And it is even less likely that these three conditions are met, the *only time* that this thought was ever formulated in my mind. Trying to explain what I don't understand would be futile. However, I could add a good five other precognitive events I experienced (such as seeing a man jumping from behind a van in front of my car seconds before he did) which at the time of writing this book can at best be interpreted as premonition. I wouldn't be surprised if a few decades from now, neuroscience will crack this phenomenon, and label it a *'seventh sense'* of some sort (that could be either fully integrated or actionable on demand).

In the meantime, it is worth training the mind to distinguish between search for excitement that leads to false intuitions and what cannot be rationally explained and is worth journaling with accuracy.

෴

4. ASLEEP BEHIND THE WHEEL

Mind conditioning might be as old as the mind itself. A familiar voice pitch, a forgotten smell, a song can plunge us into a state of excitement, sadness, anger or even *'emotional blackout'* in a split second. We are powerless to see any of it coming, it just happens. The subconscious mind operates at super high speed and without our permission. As per our thoughts, emerging out of nowhere, their traveling in and out of our mind creates a sense of ownership over them, though we are incapable to justify their provenance, analyse their impact or predict any. The claim of *seventy thousand thoughts* processed daily seems plausible but high. I think that a conservative estimate of seven thoughts per minute is realistic and since we also process thoughts during our sleep, factoring in that rate across a twenty-four-hour period suggests a guideline of about *ten thousand thoughts* a day (or seven thousand if we discount an eight-hour sleeping time). That is still a staggering number although many thoughts are duplicates to form patterns, which favours the mind's job of *sorting* and *prioritising*, known as *'DDG'* (*deleting, distorting* and *generalising*) to cope with volume and help us process a multitude of situations.

Co-existence between humans relies on the willingness to co-operate by the majorities. Tribe members, urban citizen, prison inmates, spiritual fellows all follow codes and rules to coexist. Lawful and civil behaviour is subject to consequences such as reputational damage, legal penalties, or even physical retaliation in rougher environments. For some, altruism towards the greater good of the community and social peer pressure are enough to incentivise an appropriate behaviour. Thus, we assimilate rules until they become everyday life habitual foundations that we barely notice. Just like the more we drive, the less we are aware that we're driving, as if the vehicle drove itself (for perplexed readers of the future; self-driving cars are here but still under scrutiny and not yet on the roads). Although abiding the law or driving our car feels like a no-brainer (literally), it is always the result of automated subconscious decisions of the mind. Just like *most decisions we make.* Let's turn this car imagery into an analogy; we conduct much of our life the way we drive our car: with fuel in the tank and most often on autopilot. If our body is the car body, our vital organs, the engine, our mind would be the GPS. As *'life vehicle'* however, for no apparent reason, we take unpredictable turns, drift off-track to end up in uncomfortable, often painful situations, wondering how we got there. As if driving asleep behind the wheel. Looking in hindsight, we can legitimately wonder why our *'life GPS'* is failing us. *"Why did I drop out of school? Why did I become a doctor? Why didn't I? What's my self-awareness like? Why the procrastinating? The hyperactivity?*

Whether you find these interrogations thought-provoking, irritating, pointless or meaningful, my contention is that two broader interrogations are worth focusing on, for they can mark the start of reorienting a life trajectory: *'how is my 'life driving?'* and *'who is behind the wheel?'.*

Mind Conditioning, Washing and Cleansing
Before getting into it, I want to outline three types of mind conditioning I have identified;

I) healthy (brain cleansing)
II) necessary (acclimatising)
III) unhealthy (brain washing).

I) Healthy mind conditioning (brain cleansing) might be a routine breathing exercise that makes your journey to work easier, jotting down on paper the steps of a difficult conversations you are about to have, never looking at your smartphone in the morning before a shower and your first coffee, reciting mantras or prayers that make you feel grounded and serene before climbing into bed or starting the day. Healthy routines often work.

II) Necessary mind conditioning is done in reaction to or, in preparation for events and situations we are not willing or supposed to put ourselves through. Learning how to survive and exist in jail or enduring domestic violence for example requires intensive necessary conditioning. The same is true about a challenging working environment for which you must condition your mind to accept the behaviour of certain people who you can't avoid dealing with. A less gloomy example might be preparing to face a self-imposed, ten-degree Celsius temperature winter swim in a cold lake (I am sure some of you would rather be bullied in the office, but I promise you this is so much healthier and fun!). You are about to condition yourself to hit cold water. Using your mind, you are going to prepare your entire body for it. Slow your breathing down and begin to visualise (which paradoxically, works best with the eyes closed) your tummy as a log-stuffed iron stove, non-stop heat generator: the heat is slowly spreading throughout your body, through the back of your head all the way up to the tip of your skull. You now project yourself for impact into the cold water, and a steady acclimation shortly after the initial thermal shock. You visualise yourself moving in the water, swimming stroke after stroke, propelled with continuous warm energy from the heat-inducing tummy fuelling the body, all the way down your fingertips and your toes. Open your eyes. You are ready to plunge. And off you go!

The second time around, cold water swimming will be easier because you know that you can do it, your anticipation and fears will be less intense or even gone. Which means less to worry about and less to process for the mind. The third time is even easier and before you know it, you have become a cold-water swimmer, without any training besides mind training. That's how I have been doing it for years and I can promise you that I like my showers hot. Cold temperature swimming is mostly mind over matter conditioning.

III) Unhealthy mind conditioning is the planting of unconscious routines keeping one stuck in loopy mindsets negatively altering our mood and tricking our sense of reality as a result. If you sweep your *Twitter* feed in search of antagonistic posts, are obsessed with *'likes'* on your *Instagram* account, keep over working a sore muscle at the gym, hang out with people you don't really relate to, in places where you don't feel comfortable going, you are conditioning yourself to endure things which, over time are altering your personality.

One of the perverse effects of the acclimation to discomfort is becoming prone to emotional strain. The body accommodating negative feelings and adapting to their repetition enables physiological memory to build up (in our body and in the brain) and form the fecund terrain for various compulsive behaviours to develop.

Why are we letting this take place?

5. FAKE NEWS WE TELL OURSELVES

We don't believe most of the -now proverbial- fake news. But every now and then we might be fooled. We'll be fooled at least once. But we will always be fooled by the ones we manufacture. No stories are more powerful than stories we tell ourselves.

As articulated with mind boggling clarity by Yuval Harari, believing in common stories is fundamental to the collaboration across human organisms; the story of money, corporations, the story of *God* etc...The fiction we believe in, described by Harari, taps into the same mythology exploited by the unconscious to make us feel a sense of identity and purpose. And it is made all the easier by our native, built-in tendency to cross the '*I am what I feel*' bridge, rather rapidly. Fake news we tell ourselves branch out from three phenomena of the mind.

I) The first, is self-*identification to thoughts*. Some thoughts become feelings, some of which help forging part of our identity. Feeling amazing, terrible, low, high, has nothing to do with who we are. Identification to our thoughts is how one falls off the cliff from say, guilt, into the abyss of shame. Feeling guilt comes from thinking that '*I made a mistake*' whereas shame is the result of thinking that '*I am a mistake*'. Easy to tell the difference while reading these lines but tell that to your unconscious when it is triggered by emotions overriding your rational thinking and overheating your brain at supersonic speed. Mote that such observation also applies to pleasant feelings. As much as they matter (to us), feelings are mostly the product of our thoughts and a baseless source of evidence around which to anchor our sense of identity. Feelings must be acknowledged but filtered through reasoning, to avoid distorted interpretations. Thus, identifying with ephemeral, constantly changing feelings isn't a good plan. Note that the antidote to shame and feeling shameful is not feeling shameless but feeling shame-free. If shame is one your mind's regular abusers, recognise it, then aim for a shame-free life. You'll be glad you did.

II)   The second area to watch out for is the realm of *false memories*. These aren't lies, but distorted memories, that we could swear, are accurate and legitimate. Their role is typically, to add coherence to an overall story that our mind misunderstood or that our ego couldn't deal with. As a result, the event is recorded inaccurately as a false memory, by the mind and stored as such within our '*subconscious archive*'. Thus, based on the associations the brain needed or was able to make, at the time it processed the event, it will reshape and alter characters, colours, the architecture of a place. And more importantly will also modify any unpleasantness the ego *chose* to erase. False memories are a bit like cement to fortify bricks of an overall structure to enable it to withstand the test of time, some cracks can be observed, and they usually lead somewhere that needs fixing and caring. It is quite common to uncover false memories during *guided regression* under hypnosis; memories that are believed to be true at first but later disproved, while revisiting past events and collecting the clues to piece together what really happened.

III)   The third *danger* zone where self-made fake news proliferate is the *convictions zone*. Pay attention to emotional attachment to anchorage platforms (superstition, religion, politics, sports, conspiracy theories etc...) triggers our reaction when it is challenged. Why would a flat-earther take offence at hearing that our planet is spherical, and NASA isn't hiding evidence of earth being flat? Why can't a devout Christian stand the thought that Jesus and his dad are make-belief characters that only exist in adult fairy tale books dressed up as divine wisdom? The short answer is self-identification to personal beliefs. Some thoughts become beliefs, then convictions, then foundational of the self. Meaning that, we really are *what we think*! I believe (not yet a conviction!) that we must keep our convictions in check, as hinted by American novelist Ambrose Bierce: *'convictions are variable; to be always consistent is to be sometimes dishonest'*.

A Jewish saying, with a stoicism flair, carries tempering wisdom which can help avoid fruitless debates over feelings and convictions: *'when you are happy don't be too happy and when you are unhappy don't be too unhappy'*. Failing to apply moderation to convictions we entrench ourselves in, means searching for corrupt confirmation bias to legitimise the fake news we tell ourselves. These subsequently become justification for unconscious protections we erect against imaginary threats, unreasonably tight *circles of trust* we draw around us, and one of the great misnomers of our time: our *comfort zones*.

6. FROM COMFORT ZONE TO COMFORT JAIL

Besides handling the mind's autopilot mode, the subconscious also mediates (read: *'controls'*) our decision-making process and cheers when we create routines and repetitive choices until they become second nature (some of which ultimately weave into the self-identification fabric).

Now that the car driving analogy has run its course, picture yourself seating at a sushi bar with dishes turning around the conveyor belt loop. Also, imagine sushi being new to you, no known food allergy and money being no object, so you could have anything you wanted. In that context, checking out the menu, tasting bites of everything on the belt and choosing what you liked might sound like a reasonable approach. As well as staying away from something you didn't like or something that made you feel uneasy. In practice however, novelty and opportunities tend to trigger an urge to follow a dual pathway: rapidly define *comfort zones* and create routines around them. Even if that means settling for less, like hanging in joints, we don't like much, food binging in the company of people we team with, during shopping 'therapy' raids, trying to deal with yet another week in a job we resent. Unhealthy routines are akin to hiding in some of our dysfunctionalities or even hiding in some of our functionalities, which reinforces even further the illusion that this is healthy for me. The mind's capacity to promote self-numbing in order to cope with discomfort cannot be overestimated. And now, the unprecedented era of individualistic instant-gratification enabled by exponentially fabulous technology is a hugely fecund terrain for comfort zones of solitary confinement to form.

You're smarter than your smartphone, but your smartphone knows you better than you know yourself. It can already analyse and cross-reference your shopping habits, your friends, your job, where you eat, communities you belong to, who you bank with, where you travel to, games you play and all your entertainment preferences. Very soon, tech will tell you when and why to pay a visit to the doctor and it will prioritise messages you should read, blur those you should avoid, tell you what to eat and play the best music for you, based on your sugar levels, heart rate and current mood. Such real time mood optimisation should surprise us at first, but only a little since we are already deep in constant mind washing to keep up with accelerating technological change, for our own good of course. Evidence that we should always *listen to our tech* will become too overwhelming to resist, even if it robs us of what is left of our freewill (if it ever was free) in the process. Technology is permanently altering the way we condition the mind, to think less on the one hand, and build higher expectations on the other. We used to visit shops, meet-up spontaneously, wait patiently for one another's turns while playing board games and watch a TV in groups. Today we happily tap on a screen in isolation, to order anything we want delivered the next day, food in the next hour, compulsively swipe for hollow dates, play multiple word puzzle games with perfect strangers and can't fast forward the *YouTube* clips we binge on, as soon as we get bored or restless, sheltered in the morbid comfort of remoteness. The digital revolution has made it too easy to surrender our thinking to an artificial intelligence that 'knows best'. And it does.

Rolling into our comfort zone has never been so tempting and accessible, powered with infinite options of attention displacement to deal with any discomfort. Thus, we are handing the '*A.I. God*' a free pass to deal with our anxieties and compulsions. That could mean no less than forsaking our freewill to rest in the palm of an almighty digital hand through a device that we hold in the palm of ours. Dwelling in my comfort zone:

- supports my belief that I belong somewhere
- might not be great, but it feels familiar
- also feels somehow uncomfortable
- alienates me from alternatives

Comfort zones reflect our low self-awareness, self-indoctrination, and low self-esteem. We also tend to ignore the -often significant- opportunity cost incurred when trading off our well-being for short term perceived comfort. This '*settling too quick for too little*' mindset is why we overlook the '*good stuff*' at the *life sushi table*, when we:

- *pick a healthy dish again* (self-care)
- *ditch a bad dish* (breaking bad habits)
- *cook and share food* (connect with others)
- *grab the menu beyond the belt* (self-awareness)

We instead go for what feels familiar but often leads to unhealthy and baffling choices, like when we:

- *gulp down as much as we can* (binging)
- *not pick a dish* (procrastinate)
- *let others pick for us and try to like what we're being handed* (self-abandonment)
- *choose a bad dish again* (self-sabotage)

Is the *sushi table* trying to tell us something by presenting us the same dishes over and over? Why settle for less? I believe selling ourselves short is the price we pay for our comfort zone.

A perhaps more pressing question to ask beyond *'why the bad decisions'* is *'why the comfort zone?'*. A comfort zone helps to cope with discomfort and emotional pain. As we will see with the *cognitive dissonance* phenomenon, the comfort zone is a space in which we cope with a reality that disturbs us and helps rationalise things that aren't aligned with the *'life mythology'* we follow. Of course, there is such thing as a healthy comfort zone, where reason, balance, and wisdom confine. Here's a club for a happy few, which I personally aspire to become a member of one day. If such a healthy comfort zone is already familiar to you, strive to make it your default headspace, if you haven't done so yet. Then please share with us how you did it, while the rest of us indulge in the spiritual desert of our *comfort zones*. A rather unpolished but explicit expression sums up this chapter on comfort zones in a few words, doing it much better than I could in a thousand: *"shit stinks but it's warm"*. A *discomfort* zone would seem to be a more appropriate label.

So, the *comfort zone* is one hell of a misnomer if ever any... (another one was artificial *'intelligence'*, a topic for another time and another book). Whilst the proverbial safe space or safe place grant the benefit of perceived safety, comfort zones are often home grown and self-imposed mental jail cell, keeping the mind captive, despite its door being wide open. It is no less than the adverse force preventing us from doing those things we wish we had done, the missed opportunities of the past that we reminisce about from the (dis)comfort of our death bed.

This *comfort jail* is run by the same entity keeping us *'asleep behind the wheel'*. Time to meet your oldest worst enemy and soon-to-be new best mate: the unconscious mind.

INSIDE THE MIND

INSIDE THE MIND
7. THE CONSCIOUSNESS ICEBERG

One of Oscar Wilde's insightful quotes sums up the conundrum in which human needs and wishes are enshrined: *'there are only two tragedies in life: one is not getting what one wants, and the other is getting it.'* Another quote (either authored or echoed) by Professor Gabor Maté matters a lot in my view; *'fundamentally, two things can go wrong in childhood: one is things that happen that shouldn't happen, and the other are things that should happen but don't'*. The former is about trauma, abuse and abandonment. The latter is about emotional deprivation referred to as *'proximal abandonment'* by Allan Shore.

The most fitting imagery to help picture the mind remains the popular *iceberg* cliché, with its smaller emerged, conscious visible tip and a much larger, submerged, subconscious (below the water surface) and unconscious (even deeper) invisible body. If the conscious mind is your everyday *GPS*, the more complex subconscious would be the mainframe, running 24/7 relentlessly, even during our sleep and the unconscious a sort of root archive storing foundational information which is tapped in by the subconscious to process our behaviour.

To make conceptualising it easier, I detailed below this two-phased process through which the subconscious moulds the mind and subsequently operates our decisions.

I) **Foundation Phase**: build the sense of identity
- record and archive occurrences (*what*, *where*)
- allocate meanings and gradients of importance to these occurrences and create associations between various data points (*mind mapping*)
- build beliefs about the world (*where am I*)
- connect beliefs to craft the self (*who I am*)
- develop coping strategies around beliefs (how can *'who I am'* deal with *'where I am'*)
- self-identify with core beliefs (*how things must work for 'who I am' to cope with 'where I am'*)

II) **Post-foundation phase**: affirm or reject beliefs
- monitor, record, and archive all occurrences
- keep emotional pain away
- propagate denial when necessary to alleviate the pain, at the cost of distorting reality
- support choices in line with foundation phase (*confirmation bias*)
- reject choices unaligned with foundation phase (*cognitive dissonance*)
- block or grant access to the *'unbiased ledger'* within the unconscious, higher self (our chance to *'choose again'* during guided regression)

A key dimension of the unconscious is its capacity to manipulate beliefs we're unaware of but connected to. We go about, not paying attention to the impact that our feelings yield upon our lives and uncurious of why we feel the way we feel. If you feel good most of the time, finding out why you do may not be a priority, but if you experience recurrent anxiety, discomfort, phobias and repeat negative patterns, you ought to take a trip down into your untapped unknown unconscious.

Known unknown and unknown unknown

Imagine that you have gone on a diet because you felt the need to lose weight. Here you have an idea of what your so-called '*known unknown*' is; you know that you must lose weight (*known*). You just don't know yet how many pounds you need to shed (*unknown*) to reach your objective (of aesthetic, kinaesthetic or clinical nature).

But if you were overweight in a world where everyone was overweight, unaware that weight was affecting your wellbeing, then you wouldn't be thinking of losing weight because you wouldn't know it was an option. Let alone that you had to do something about it: that is the '*unknown unknown*'.

Denial

At its core, it is a form of protection deployed by the subconscious ego to reinforce beliefs and accept or refuse reality. Prime examples are found in environments favourable to fecund irrationality, rampant contradictions and offensively inaccurate claims (usual suspects we have already touched on):

- *politics*: doubling down despite evidence that electing the indefensible was a terrible mistake.
- *oil lobbies*: putting profits before public health.
- *family*: a mother turning a blind eye to evidence that her child committed terrible things.
- *domestic violence*: a woman engulfed in emotional abuse telling herself that the rage-oholic she married is changing and the beating will cease.
- *religion*: despite being the almighty creator of all (that would include *Satan*) *God* is utterly powerless to stop suffering and evil on earth.

At a time of '*hyper information*', when ignorance has become a choice, is denial a sign of ignorance, or stupidity? Absolutely not. Just like not being in denial isn't a sign of knowledge, or of intelligence (but a sign of awareness). Denial is a mental failure to face the truth and compromise instead, to either; hang on to what we have, get what we want, or not being 'found out'. It happens to literally millions of otherwise intelligent individuals who stand up for senseless doctrines and endorse mentally sick or even imaginary individuals. Denial is an irrational force rooted in fear and emotions which can defeat our brightest intellectual faculties.

Denial goes hand in hand with what's known as *cognitive dissonance*; the mental stress experienced when holding contradictory beliefs. When confronted with revealing facts that can't be rationally argued, we look for ways to reduce the discomfort incurred, typically by withdrawing into more denial leading to a '*doubling down*', '*digging deeper*' culture of the mind.

Cognitive dissonance is a way for the mind to rationalise our world, with all its contradictions. This phenomenon is disproportionately widespread in environments that bear borderline schizophrenic, deeply ambivalent marks as observed in (I know; once again) religious indoctrination. The severe dissonance that religious believers face becomes entrenched in dogmatism. Accepting the dichotomy between an almighty caring *God* and daily horrors happening in the world, that include children dying in plane crashes or being sexually abused by no less than men of *God* themselves, is no small paradox for the mind to handle. To justify the unjustifiable -to themselves and to others- believers find refuge under a divine umbrella, in an apparent effort to shape justifications you might have heard before: '*it is proof Satan is real*', '*it is God testing our faith*', '*you must read this passage, of this particular edition of the holy book*'. Such subterfuges also come handy to (consciously or not) alleviate the guilt of sacrificing one's intellect on the altar of untenable mythology. Besides, the spiritual reflection coupled with rituals, gatherings, fraternal meals and celebrations found in organised religions understandably reinforce ties to the community and bonds between its members. Also, bear in mind that religious faith is interwoven in the believer's sense of identity, usually since early childhood. That is why an alternative truth for the believer's ego is so difficult to face; *God* is powerless (equating to '*I'm powerless*' for the believer), doesn't care ('*I am unprotected*') or isn't there at all ('*I am nothing and alone*'). And of course, it conveys a sense of betrayal -albeit involuntary- from family members and religious peers. No wonder that the minute such thoughts form, the ego takes over to bombard the mind with argumentative confirmation bias until the crisis of faith is over. Such reactions can be observed across every religion and happen in good faith (pun intended). In fact, if you are religious yourself, you might sense a slightly mind-bending discomfort as the urge to rationalise your own faith grew while reading this chapter. If that is the case, I ask you to consider that you might be experiencing *cognitive dissonance* and have rolled over into your *comfort zone*, out of necessity. Particularly, if you experience resentment (that your ego) masked into charitable feelings of compassion towards me right now, along with a prayer to wish me well. The intent here, besides illustrating how the ego manipulates our cognition is to be thought provoking rather than gratuitously provocative and I hope that it will be perceived as such by most readers, religious or not.

Denial and cognitive dissonance are like '*shadow soldiers*' serving the ego, keeping the '*unknown unknown*' invisible, buried within the unconscious. That leaves us unable to deal with an unknown *(unknown)* intruder, who we don't even know lives '*up there*'.

Therefore, it is only after the realisation and the admission of its existence that we can embark on the critical journey towards uncovering what lies beneath our '*comfort zone*'. An unfamiliar terrain that fosters much of our frustrations: the *causality of our emotional pain.*

INSIDE THE MIND
8. THE CAUSALITY OF OUR EMOTIONAL PAIN

Whilst emotions cause reactions, emotional pain causes transformation. More specifically, emotions beget reactions (including inaction), some of which will spur emotional pain. Note that emotions per se are meaningless. They acquire meaning only once the mind connects them to our belief system. For instance, witnessing someone you don't know criticise the work of someone else you also don't know, should leave you unmoved and unaffected. But if someone, whose professional opinion you respect, criticises *your* work even mildly, the emotion you will feel as a result might transform into emotional pain, particularly if your belief system has got you (read; *your-self*) identified with your work. Meanwhile, someone uninvolved, external to your situation wouldn't be emotionally affected (just as you weren't when the situation involved somebody else and not you).

Once the emotional pain has formed, it disrupts our emotional *flora* and will require transformation to cope. For instance: '*a comment I received made me feel incompetent, bruised my self-esteem and as a result I am in emotional pain. I feel a sense of uselessness growing into a void, which I need to fill with something*'. That is where the need for *compensation* and a *coping strategy* arises, usually in the form of proactive reaction (*fight to disprove*), passive inaction (*paralysis*) or active retraction (*isolation*). As we saw earlier, to endure and deal with pain, the subconscious builds compensatory fortresses like the *comfort zone*, part of a broader '*mythology mainframe*' aiming to rationalise pain and allocate it a meaning, albeit fictitious.

Somebody said that most things we do in life are either an act of love, or a cry for love. That certainly resonates when looking at children, even more so with infants. Having just landed, they are binary, love giving and receiving beings, rather unprepared for anything else. Having no concept of the world yet, the initial perception of our child self is that the world is us or at the very least that it revolves around us, enabled by parents often acting around us as if it is so. It is therefore common for children to feel in control of situations, outcomes and the well-being of people around them. Children feel emotions at face value, provide unfiltered feedback and aren't prepped for events disrupting their routines and their nascent, fragile forming belief system. They are busy making sense of the tiny kingdom over which they rule as the *King*-like narcissistic figures they are. It is no surprise that the emotional confusion and discomfort felt by a child tends to be blown out of proportions (and of course, it can also be justified by any standard, depending on circumstances).

Consider two distinctive examples; a six-year-old being left on his own for three minutes at an airport lounge and another six-year-old, used to never being picked up after school. Although the difference in gravity between the two situations should be obvious, both children can experience a similar level of emotional suffering of neglect and abandonment. The one subject to the repetition of not being picked up at school should experience a deeper feeling of not being worthy of attention than the one being neglected for a few minutes at the airport. However, the mark of the trauma left can be harmful and long lasting for both, if it created the illusion, albeit brief, that they had been abandoned.

As adults, both individuals will naturally no longer be thinking of these episodes and yet they might still be unconsciously connected to them. Unaware of being under the influence of a life-long mythology they formed over time, in reaction to events they did not understand and couldn't process rationally at the time. Our native level of sensitivity also plays a big role in how we let past events impact us emotionally.

For instance, should the child who has only been left unattended for a few minutes at the airport be biologically more sensitive than the other child (being left to come home from school on his own) he might experience more complications as an adult. The greater the sensitivity, the greater the pain and the greater the resulting strategies to cope. Hence, the importance of becoming aware of the *coping mythology* we created during childhood.

INSIDE THE MIND
9. CREATING OUR COPING MYTHOLOGY

If you were reading a film script this would be the '*point of no return*' part. If properly articulated, this chapter might trigger a new habit of second guessing why you do things you do, say the things you say, and (for the bravest lot) *think the thoughts you think*. You might even catch yourself wondering the same about others around you (evidently a lost cause, but I can think of worse ways to kill time).

False beliefs can be viewed as both a blessing and a curse, a force for survival but also an ill-fitted lens to assess opportunities and make decisions. I don't think that the impact of deep-rooted beliefs on shaping the life we end up living is understood enough. I suspect that untreated unconscious beliefs beget self-imposed restraint and unwarranted emotional misery for millions. In some ways, unconscious beliefs are more difficult to expel than the religious beliefs that shape a child's view of the world before they are given a chance to form a critical mind. Whilst the adult, breaking away from religion typically faces a backlash and judgement from community and family members, at least the roots of the beliefs can be traced back and identified (to religious beliefs being forced upon them as a child). Whereas there is no way to trace back unconscious beliefs that are the product of specific interpretation we manufactured during childhood. Not consciously. They are out of reach. *Purposely* buried in the unconscious. More importantly, as we saw earlier, we are not even aware that we are unaware of those beliefs, bullying our mental well-being. In other words: *we are unaware that we are unaware that we have been hijacked*.

How do I face an adverse force keeping my mind hostage if I am unaware of its existence? Meet your own *unknown unknown*. I picked a few quotes to help pondering over this critical aspect:

- '*It is hard to fight an enemy who has outposts in your head*' (Sally Kempton),
- '*We often give our enemies the means for our own destruction*' (Aesop),
- '*Love your enemies; for they shall tell you all your faults*' (Benjamin Franklin)
- '*Know your enemy and know yourself and you can fight a hundred battles without disaster*' (Sun Tzu),
- '*To make peace with the enemy, work with him till he becomes a partner*' (Nelson Mandela).

To get a sense of where this is going, replace the word 'enemy' with the word '*ego*' in the above quotes. Since most of our life is defined by our choices, I believe that it is crucial to find out why we make some of the choices we make or rather; *what* is making them for us. It is perfectly obvious that most people follow common sense, don't take life-threatening risks, don't do drugs, neither smoke nor use violence etc... But when it comes to other, seemingly harmless decisions, I would argue that most people have limited knowledge *if any*, as to why they left or stayed in their hometown, voted for their president, married their spouse etc... Particularly if we try to benchmark these choices against our self-awareness (or lack thereof). If answered honestly, the question: '*are my decisions in line with my principles and what I know to be working in favour of my well-being?*' can change the course of a life trajectory.

How many times, do we see someone rush to remarry right after a divorce, insist on working in jobs that keep them miserable and hang out in places they don't like? Beyond conformism, it has to do with low self-awareness fostering unhealthy choices leading to compensatory compulsive behaviours, from shopping splurges, food binging to full-on gambling, sex, drug and alcohol addictions. Whilst therapists tend to swiftly pack these so-called disorders into the depression suitcase, an alternative is to trace back to the root cause and eradicate them for good, by way of a *'look again, choose again'* method. I met grown-ups convinced they were born depressed, cursed, insignificant, doomed to fail, destined to succeed, meant to be wealthy, meant to be average, meant to be this and that...*Does it matter*? It matters a lot. Because we can and do shape our fate's trajectory channelling our mind power, the architect of the *coping mythology* built on *fake news we tell ourselves*.

Whilst *'remarriage is the triumph of hope over experience'* for Oscar Wilde, it is probably also the triumph of subconscious cognition over rationality. I recently encountered a real-life example of buried past motives driving present pathology; somebody who witnessed an uncle have a fatal heart attack when they were seven years of age and remembered the incident as an adult. She had forgotten that at the time of the tragedy, the uncle was carrying groceries that fell crashing on the ground. That led the unprepared seven-year-old to associate food with death and develop a severe, life-threatening eating disorder as a result later in life. Such association was uncovered by tracing back to its causality and an awfully specific emotional trauma.

By leaving such a stone unturned, with each year passing, the subconscious reinforced an unsolicited and unnecessary protective shield, in reaction to the emotional pain endured while coping poorly and, in this case, affecting gravely someone's eating habits.

And thus, life-long false beliefs invented by the ego are enacted and grown, until they become life-defining foundation and *pillars of our sense of identity*.

INSIDE THE MIND
10. PILLARS OF OUR SENSE OF IDENTITY

Debating the question *'who am I'* is a rather futile initiative. I found that instead, narrowing down the guess work through elimination by asking *'who am I not'* turned out be a lot more productive.

However, deconstruction isn't on the *ego's to-do list* since it is all about constructing certainties around firm beliefs, albeit often false. To forge our sense of self and identity, the subconscious ego processes all the external data gathered during our interactions with the outside world and particularly with our immediate environment. We stress test our sense of self trying to address interrogations such as; *'does surrounding myself with individuals of perceived good reputation make me a person of good reputation? Does spending time with dubious individuals mean I am a bad egg myself?'* What is verifiable beyond doubt, is that over time, surroundings and repetition impact our character, our beliefs, our convictions, and our decisions.

Seemingly forever, humans have felt the urge to belong, to fit in and the need to sort one another with labels and terms that facilitate associations: *'he is an accountant; he must be boring but reliable'*, *'she is a singer; she won't be on time but she should be fun to hang out with once she shows up'*, *'homosexuals are wealthy'*, *'he grew up poor, he can't be the sharpest knife in the drawer'*. As generic and offensive as they are, prejudices belong to centuries of pre-formed ideas based on perception that led to generalisation. How we perceive others and ourselves (read: *our self*) moulds the beliefs and the convictions we end up condemning or identifying with. Tragically, bias and self-fulfilling prophecies of racial causality towards behaviour and intelligence are still rampant in our societies. Young adults from certain ethnic minorities growing up in poor suburbs are still being told how statistically doomed they are. And sadly, they allow the perception of others (including older fatalist neighbours) to affect their intellectual potential and personal development. Meanwhile the *'intellectually superior Asians'* from affluent families would be thriving effortlessly in life. Ghetto kids would be less smart than kids from posher suburbs or different ethnicities. *Hell no*! These children end up verifying such morbid self-fulfilling statistics (which of course, consolidate the bias further) only because they are made to feel hopeless. Undoubtedly, in alternative realities, some of these kids would be on their way to become scholars, lawyers, doctors, and scientists, instrumental in fixing climate change or curing the world of cancer (or even, of *wokism*, one can always dream). Ghetto kids aren't at war, but they feel as if they were, spending most of their energy in survival mode, which often translates into violence for which they end up jailed or dead. Who is still failing to understand that a brain saturated with constant emotional repression cannibalises any chance to focus on the ordinary business of doing homework? As is often the case, change to fix such revolting vicious spiral doesn't come from politicians, but from individuals who walk the walk, like *NBA* superstar Lebron James, who I would, despite the absence of religious props in my life, shamelessly brand an *'icon'*. Lebron is changing the course of history and statistics in his former neighbourhood with a magnificent initiative to give back and show what 'not forgetting where one comes from' looks like (*Google*: *'Akron school opening'*).

Rather than wondering who we are and what others think of us, a better use of our time, might be to reflect upon the question *'why the need for the label and the tribe?'* Our primal need to belong for survival, also addresses partially the root of our subliminal fear of abandonment. Before building a sense of *public* identity, the ego builds a sense of *individual* identity, based on perceptions of our potential, our limits, sense of purpose (or lack thereof) and our place in this world. One of my patients once told me that he was born unworthy of attention. He knew that for a fact. We found out during regression that, as a child, being repeatedly ignored or dismissed by evasive parents created a sense of invisibility. It later turned into a belief, which he ultimately identified with: *'mum and dad aren't paying attention to me'.* It made him feel unworthy of attention*: 'I must be invisible'.* This patient reacted (to emotional depravation having caused the belief of unworthiness and identification to invisibility) by becoming as visible as he could, with a career in acting and then in TV. Regressive therapy unbundled two core *false beliefs*: that he is unworthy of attention, and that he was born that way. As trivial as these beliefs might seem to the adult, they meant the world to him as a child and drove the course of his life. Not all are under the impression that they were born doomed, but all were unconsciously subject to adversarial stealth beliefs operating under the radar. In other words, most patients believed that their fate was sealed but they weren't aware of it (*'unknown unknown'* at work). Whilst the concept of lifelong *false beliefs* should be easy to grasp, its successor *'Pillars of our Sense of Identity'* could do with a more detailed, step by step breakdown, from *event* to *identification*:

- **Event** (different examples, same outcome):
    1) a child is left unattended for three minutes
    2) a child is never picked up after school
    3) a child is being ignored at home
- Event begets **trauma**: fright and abandonment
- Trauma begets **false belief**: '*I am unworthy of attention*'.
- False belief becomes **identification**: '*I am invisible*'
- Identification begets **reaction**: to either *validate* in submission, or *invalidate* in rebellion, the belief that '*I'm unworthy of attention*' that leads to identify as '*I'm invisible*'.
- Reaction begets **self-indoctrination**: creating or being drawn to situations that will validate the narrative I created (submit or rebel).
- Self-indoctrination becomes **default behaviour**: crafting a life path around the self-indoctrination I inflict on myself.

In this case, I become either:

I) a *reclusive, librarian, trouble free member of society*, if I chose to validate in submission, to the *false belief* that I am unworthy of attention and the ensuing *identification* to someone '*invisible*',

or, at the other end of the spectrum.

II) I chose to infirm that same *false belief* in a rebellious effort, and I go on to become an *extrovert, attention craving TV presenter* who can't get enough media coverage.

Note that (and see why below), in both cases, regardless of the chosen path, the individual will keep on feeling '*invisible*'.

Two key points from this sequence:

I)   The *self-indoctrination* (a form of self-fulfilling prophecy thrown at destiny) is the subconscious, shaping our sense of identity behind our backs. It is what drives one to behave as either a shy introvert, because '*I don't matter and I am invisible*', or on the other hand, behave as an '*over the top*' extrovert always looking to steal the show, also because '*I don't matter and I am invisible*'. Neither of these behaviours will do anyone any good since they are neither an expression, nor a reflection of who we are and thus create an imbalanced sense of identity often leading to depression.

II)   The *reaction to false beliefs* (in this case that '*I'm not worthy of attention*') leading to self-indoctrination is an attempt by the ego to deal with a situation it didn't understand in the first place. As per the aforementioned examples, what happened was that a child was left unattended for three minutes by loving parents or ignored at home or never being picked up at school by parents who perhaps were too stressed out or not wealthy enough to provide the necessary care. What didn't happen was parents telling their child that they found them unworthy of attention which is why they planned on abandoning them so that they could feel invisible. However, false beliefs do anchor within, and even when the reaction is to fight to disprove the belief that our ego created ('*unworthy of attention*'), it leaves the sense of identity unchanged i.e. that '*I don't matter, and I am invisible*'. In other words, no matter how hard that man who went on to become a TV host tried to surround himself with attention, he constantly failed the validation test because he did it in reaction to a distorted belief ('*I am invisible*') that was never going to leave its foothold. And thus, he still felt invisible at the top of his career, which came to an end due to depression that had become unmanageable. Simply put; *if we treat the symptoms the cause remains within*.

If I become a celebrity *to run away from feeling invisible*, I am still going to feel *invisible* because I haven't reconnected to the inception, i.e. when that deep-rooted *false belief* formed. That means going all the way back to the event(s) that triggered the trauma around which I built a false sense of identity (that shaped most of my thinking through my adult life). A good hundred other examples could illustrate the dynamics of identification. Here are a few cases I encountered:

- a five-year-old girl unintentionally spills milk, mum calls her *useless*. As an adult she became a professional athlete, the youngest partner in a *Big Four* consulting firm, a multi-millionaire and aged forty-three contemplated suicide because of *how useless* she feels.
- a man who grew up being routinely beaten up and emotionally abused by his parents became a heavy drug user as a teen, got clean as a grown-up, became a sober life evangelist but also a compulsive *S&M fetish 'submissive'* and a violent father to act out both as a victim and as the abuser (a classic, albeit tragic *'victim triangle'* case).

What if I told you, that someone else who grew up in a family of emotionally distant lawyers and judges became a criminal, simply to receive attention from judges and lawyers as a grown-up?!

And in case you find any of these far-fetched and wonder how someone who spilt milk as a toddler ends up suicidal because of it, or becomes a criminal

to meet judges, note that these aren't the most
severe cases I have encountered. As you have no
doubt figured out; it isn't the *event itself* but the
child's *interpretation* of emotional distraught that
causes the irrational behaviour. The subsequent
actions undertaken (become an over-achiever) to
invalidate the false belief (that '*I am useless*') won't
change a sense of identity that has been anchored
and subconsciously fed for decades with a narrative,
which in this case, was '*I will prove mum, at any cost,
that I am not useless*'. It is fair to wonder though, why
her success didn't make her feel better about
herself. Every achievement reminded her why she
chased them in the first place, during inner
unconscious chats that went along those lines:

> Self: '*I won a medal.*'
> Ego: '*You won a medal?*'
> Self: '*I won a medal.*'
> Ego: '*What did you win a medal for?*'
> Self: '*To be the best*'
> Ego: '*Why be the best?*'
> Self: '*To feel good about myself*'
> Ego: '*Oh, good... And do you?*'
> Self: '*I suppose so. Well...not really*'
> Ego: '*Why not?*'
> Self: '*I have felt useless for so long...*'
> Ego:'*Right; you're useless, no matter what.*'
> Self: '*I guess...*'

No matter how much we achieve, *how we feel
about ourselves deep down is connected to what
happened during childhood.* Hence the importance of
'*reconnecting to the past to connect the dots.*' That
would be why it'll be easier to unbundle religious
beliefs than unconscious ones. Whilst religious

beliefs will be harder to part with because of peer pressure, they will be easier to unbundle, while unconscious beliefs will be easier to part with but harder to unbundle.

I couldn't conclude this crucial chapter more eloquently than by repeating a brilliant *Jungian* quote: *'Until you make the unconscious conscious it will direct your life and you will call it fate.'*

MAKE THE EGO YOUR *AMIGO*

MAKE THE EGO YOUR *AMIGO*
11. YOUR EGO IS NOT YOUR *AMIGO*!

It is wise to review the *self* before discussing the ego. The self can be split into twin selves:

I)   The *original/higher self*: fear-free, acting for our well-being. Think of it as inner clarity that can be tap into, so long as we know how to access it.

II)   The *coping self*: unaware victim of unconscious fears instated and fed by the ego, enduring states such as frustration, stagnation, confusion, low self-esteem, and lack of purpose.

A turning point in my life was managing to connect the *coping self* to my *original self* and realign them according to their respective roles. It felt like freeing the mind from a ton of bricks I had been dragging everywhere I went, for decades. I found out these were mostly burdens littered by the ego, which would also distract and prevent me from dealing with real threats. To understand the ego, I must first point out that all that is kept away from our conscious reach isn't acting against us, far from it. Let's look at definitions according to various sources. For the *Cambridge Dictionary*, the ego is '*a person's sense of self-esteem and self-worth*'. In philosophy and metaphysics, it's '*a conscious thinking subject*'. In Psychoanalysis it is '*the part of the mind that mediates between the conscious and the unconscious and is responsible for reality testing and a sense of personal identity*'. And as per the Axel's *Life Dictionary*, the ego is '*a self-proclaimed benevolent dictator, fake news propagator of a distorted narrative and dispatcher of unsolicited protection against imaginary threats.*'

As we have touched on earlier, those imaginary threats are created in reaction to events that occurred during childhood. *My ego campaigns for sanctions based on interpretations it attached to my belief system until they become integral part of my sense of identity.* It will keep on bullying the mind *to validate and affirm these sanctions until they become anchored beliefs and rules governing my thought and decision process.* In other words, the ego's default setting is to assign a sense of identity and feed the mind a narrative (rooted in interpretations of episodes experienced as traumatic) that accidentally block our growth and expansion.

Hence, the importance of keeping in mind (and on a fridge magnet) another pertinent and critical Jungian quote: '*I am not what happened to me*'.

To summarise the dynamic of the triangle formed by *coping self,* the *original self,* and the *ego*; the *coping self* is a '*faulty GPS*' which the *original self* can fix by recalibrating the *ego*. Failing to work on that means failing to realise that our feelings, defined by our thoughts, are defining us. And without a conscious effort to '*think oneself into what's right for us*', we go through life unknowingly believing that we are what we think. And we become just that.

Choose your friends carefully, stay close to them, closer to your enemies maybe, but no matter what you do; *make your ego your amigo.*

MAKE THE EGO YOUR *AMIGO*
12. WE ARE NOT OUR THOUGHTS

If you have ever read or listened to *Eckhart Tolle*, you might be familiar with the claim that *we are not what we think*. If we don't pay attention (and we don't), the mind naturally associates some of our thoughts with our sense of self. *What does that mean and why does this matter?*

It means that we look at things *from* a thought instead of looking *at* our thoughts. We should look at thoughts come and go and realise that they don't really mean anything. Instead, we react to our thoughts letting them loop and become familiar to the point of integration into our mental mainframe. For example, if I keep thinking to myself *'silly me I should know better'*, over trivial occurrences not warranting self-assessment or judgement ('forgot to buy the butter', 'missed a turn driving on my way to the doctor' etc...) after a while, the mind associates this recurrent thought with my sense of self: *'I must be someone silly who should know better'*. I then embark on an unconscious search for confirmation bias by gradually behaving like someone *'silly who should know better'*, which over time, enough people will witness for my subconscious to *validate* and engrave this trait of personality into the *'mind DNA'*, where the illusions of *'what and who I am'* cocoon.

I believe it matters greatly for two reasons; I) we project someone we are not (neither want to be) and II) we compromise who we really are, which creates a life opportunity cost (often of epic proportions) by missing out on who we should be, but did not, because we were too busy becoming *someone silly who should know better*.

An efficient and simple way to deal with such a thought, next time it crosses your mind is to *pause to observe* (much like during a *'mindfulness'* routine) and realise that: *'I am having the thought that I am silly and I should know better. Another thought linked to my distorted self-esteem. It doesn't mean that I am silly. Let's move on to the next thought.'*

To get more perspective and detachment, let's take a *'silly'* self-esteem test by becoming somebody else. Pick someone (famous or not) who in your eyes, incarnates self-confidence and success. If no one comes to mind, try Beyoncé, JK Rowling, Michelle Obama, Meryl Streep, Bruce Lee, Clint Eastwood, the Dalai Lama or Michael Jordan. Pick someone who somehow resonates because you look up to them or because you just love what they do. Now imagine what it must be like to be them as they walk into a room. Wildly acclaimed by millions for major achievements. No financial worries, most things taken care of for them. Think how you would approach people you see and everything you do if you were one of the most fulfilled individuals alive on the planet. Breathe in slower, and deeper with each exhale. Close your eyes. Become that person. Walk into that room. Shoulders back, tummy tucked in, looking sideways, now looking ahead. How are you feeling? Now, fade out and crawl back into the *'silly me, should know better'* shell. How are you feeling now? Is your mind allowing you to tell the difference?

Let the undisputable fact sink in that, whoever you picked, also has terrible days and struggles with how they feel. No matter your perception of them. No one is immune to emotional pain. No matter who we are. Or who we think we are.

Don't forget that many supposedly emancipated celebrities are frequent rehab visitors and suicide isn't underrepresented within these circles. By the way, feeling suicidal is a thought that must be acknowledged very seriously. But that should also be treated for what it is, the product of our mind. Thinking of suicide means that we are *thinking of* suicide. It doesn't mean that we don't belong with the rest of us and are doomed to committing suicide. It means that *we are having these thoughts because we are feeling* trapped and helpless. We are feeling this way; it isn't this way. We feel trapped and helpless, because of thoughts, which create additional, darker thoughts, of suicide in this case. A high security prison inmate is literally, physically trapped but can choose to not feel helpless, which, by any account, is very difficult to achieve in such an environment. On the other hand, if you are thinking 'methods' to plan suicide, you have suicidal *intentions* and should definitely find the strength to reach out for help.

Extremes aside, you will see that by slowing it down, we can alter our thinking, and with repetition, get a shot at feeling differently. And just like that, we become someone else, in what feels like a new reality that we created through mind projection.

MAKE THE EGO YOUR *AMIGO*
13. YET WE *KINDA* BECOME WHAT WE THINK

If you wanted to extract mantras from this book they would be '*I am not what happened to me*' and '*I am not my thoughts*'. In fact, repeating these ten times every morning for ten days, might produce a slight positive mood change. Feel free to add to it '*I am not my job, my work, my family, my money*': labels around which our *conceptualised selves are* anchored. Our mind cultivates the past to anticipate and manage the future. We cannot change the past, but we can consciously manage present choices we are about to make. In that sense we can alter our behaviour and consequently "tomorrow's past".

The reason why, as we saw earlier, we can easily become '*someone silly who should know better*' is to fulfil one of the ego's key missions; to forge our sense of identity, at any cost since, the worst drama for the ego is to feel that the '*I*' is nobody. To affirm our identity, acquire a sense of belonging and flee loneliness, we connect, socialise, join clubs and fellowships. Once again, religion comes in handy to illustrate the *identification to belief* phenomenon. When believers mention '*my* religion, *my faith*', they refer to a crucial anchorage to which a vital sense of identity and divine purpose are attached. Granted, the alternative realisation, that mankind is a random by-product of molecular circumstances resulting in billions of us aimlessly drifting on a rock into space, isn't cool. It strips us naked, doesn't provide any metaphysical answer and takes us way out of our *comfort zone.* Meanwhile, religion provides a buffet of adjustable narratives one can cherry pick in order to justify what can't be justified rationally. In other words, choosing faith in oneself over a divine power isn't easy and means facing the vacuity of our *raison d'être* with little immediately discernible reward in exchange.

To not be accountable to a divine force isn't unspiritual; taking offence over who does so, is.

I entitled this chapter 'we "*kinda* become what we think' because I don't subscribe to the proverbial *law of attraction* bounced around so-called spiritual circles and is clearly nonsense damaging most of its adepts. I contend that the impact of thought over our behaviour and destiny must be nuanced, if only to avoid creating guilt in people for who the law of attraction "*doesn't work*" (i.e. the immense majority!).

With that in mind, I would phrase it as follows; our sense of identity is the product of our feelings and beliefs, which are themselves the product of our thoughts. It is almost impossible to feel anything, besides primal instinctive feelings, *if I am not thinking* (you will experience it for yourself in '*square breathing*' later). Since the majority of my feelings are correlated to my thinking (itself running my belief system) it is in my interest to pay attention to how my thoughts impact how I feel, which ends up shaping who I think I am, and therefore, over time, who I become and who I don't become.

With that, to hell with *LOA* evangelists!

MAKE THE EGO YOUR *AMIGO*
14. EMBARKING ON YOUR *EGOVERY*

'How heavy is a bucket half-full of muddy water?'

While you mull over the answer to that question, -which is answered two paragraphs down-, I give you, after analogies of an *iceberg*, a *GPS*, a *sushi conveyor belt* and a *supercomputer*: *the pulled muscle*, and *the artichoke* analogy. A pulled muscle that isn't healed underperforms but it still works. However, it becomes more painful over time, harder to use and to put back into shape. The same is true about the ego pulling our '*mind muscles*' sideways while attempting to shield us from it with a metaphorical armour it forged. It burdens us and becomes heavier, the older we get.

So, *'How heavy is a bucket half-full of muddy water?'* It depends how long you hold it for. Far away, silent meditative retreats may be great but utterly superfluous to identify hard-wired old beliefs holding us back. The retreat we need for sure, is the one into the *higher self* (bypassing the *coping self*) to find out and get rid of *who and what I am not*. No monastery, no praying, no affirmation, and no magic are required. It's a process. A methodical shedding and decluttering process aiming to undo what was built improperly. Unpack the distorted beliefs, the blocking thoughts and shed them one by one, as you would, *layers of an artichoke*. Acknowledging in the process that obsolete fabrications of the mind that should no longer define you. Another way to approach this '*uncover to discover and recover*' process is to say; *who, what I am, is found by peeling off all the things that I am not and never was.* Once such a process is undertaken, we can readjust our life trajectory.

As I mentioned in the *Introduction*, I purposely spent more time trying to detail the issue at length and less time on the solution by design. And the time has finally come to look at *how* we tap into the unconscious realm to make peace with the ego and fix our bugs, through guided regression.

☙❧

REGRESS TO PROGRESS

REGRESS TO PROGRESS
15. TAKING ANOTHER LOOK AT THE ICEBERG

Now that the notion of the subconscious and the unconscious that lies beneath its conscious twin has been brought to surface and to your attention, here is a brief recap to carry on into the process with optimal clarity. My focus is on the impact over our lives of what is *not conscious*, irrespective of the levels of unconsciousness. Consequently, I deliberately don't labour too much over what is *subconscious* from what is *unconscious*, which could have borne the risk of creating confusion (something I have painfully tried to avoid all along the book) rather than bring insight and answers. A lot of our burdens are false beliefs linked to past events and experienced as traumatic that the ego dealt with by feeding a distorted narrative that ended up shaping some of our choices, our sense of identity and ultimately key components of the reality we end up living in.

To understand my current behaviour, I must:
- Trace back to the *inception*: *what happened*
- Investigate the *causality*: how *what happened made me feel*
- Realise the *false identification* that occurred: how I connected *how I felt* to *who I am* (*coping self*)
- *Redefine the meaning* of what really happened and realign it to *who I am* (*original/higher self*)

I'll now unpack how to trace back to why we feel the way we do, starting with two key contextualising factors:

I) The type of phase we are going through right now has a direct impact on what we have been thinking, which has a direct impact on how we are feeling. It is much easier to undergo a guided regression therapy when we are not going through financial hardship and none of our basic needs are affected.

II) Events we went through during childhood that had a direct impact on shaping our self-perception and our ensuing sense of purpose and identity.

Now that we have looked at the *iceberg* again, it is time to take an exploratory dive within its depths.

❧

REGRESS TO PROGRESS
16. GUIDED REGRESSION: CHOOSING AGAIN

This African proverb embraces the essence of guided regression so well that here I am, quoting it a second time: '*If you don't know where you are going look where you came from*'.

Our personal history can teach us a lot about our present situation. Particularly our forgotten history. The most efficient way that I know to move on from patterns holding us back (i.e. *to progress*) is done by going back to the root causes (i.e. *to regress*). You are going to effectively '*regress to progress*' your way out of '*analysis paralysis*' and realign with who you really set out to be.

The crucial trip back to our *original self* requires *bypassing the ego*. Bypassing the ego is done by delving into a *regressive state*. Since a lot of what we feel is the product of choices we made, the notion of '*choosing again*' must be understood. Regression provides the platform to revisit past decisions outside of the emotional vacuum, with more clarity and care. A regressive state is *an altered state of consciousness during which we reconnect to our past in ways we can't access while conscious*.

෧෧෧

REGRESS TO PROGRESS
17. RECONNECT TO THE PAST TO CONNECT THE DOTS

Breakthroughs from guided regression:
- *becoming aware of who I am not*
- *becoming aware of burdens that I should shed*
- *defuse the redundant, belief system in place*
- *break free from the ego hijack, rewire my mind*

Guided regression is where we redefine the rules:
- the self takes some control back over the ego
- distorted interpretations recalibrate
- reassign healthier duties to the hyperactive ego

During most sessions and especially during the first one, our *original self* is incarnated as our *child self* (a.k.a. inner child) since the formative years of childhood is when the ego begins to intervene to deal with events registered as traumatic by the child's (child) mind.

I thought a patient-to-therapist '*Q&A*' format was best suited to walk you through how guided regression works.

What is Regression?
Regression is an altered state of consciousness granting access to past circumstances we are no longer consciously connected to. A regressive trip is very much like retrieving misplaced data from a computer's hard drive. Data which has been bugging the mind's operating system.

It is a channeling technique to explore and break the unconscious adverse (and often destructive) patterns and replace them with a new point of view about ourselves and life around us. In regression, one experiences augmented clarity and reconnects to forgotten information which has been typically, blocked off from the mind in reaction to the emotional pain caused by events we were emotionally ill equipped to deal with, and buried in the depths of our unconscious. Regardless of their amplitude, the unconscious mind brands these incidents as traumatic and locks them up, to conceal the emotional discomfort and hurt endured.

Why go back in time?

To identify the causality of our emotional pain and revisit the interpretation of past events that left a mark. By reconnecting to our *original self,* we reach the altered state of consciousness that opens the door to nature and the *impact* of past traumas, of any amplitude. It means that by delving into regression we are not treated *with*, but *in* regression.

By going back in time, we revisit and work on traumatic events, adjusting the past interpretations that led to the set of beliefs and the corrupted sense of identity that the ego created to cope with the trauma. As a direct result of an adjusted and clarified understanding of *what really happened back then, we are then able to correct our behaviour right now*. Since we are *literally* changing our mind. In other words; going back time will allow you to have a better time with yourself and with your life, going forward.

Does it work?

Yes. On willing participants i.e. individuals whose ego will let a third party '*take them under*': the state of altered consciousness required to reconnect with the *original self.* Sessions are crafted around specific issues or left to unfold. A recalibration of the mind is usually visible beyond doubt within weeks. For trust to build up with your therapist, find one you feel guided by rather than talked to. Three sessions or less are enough to erase deep rooted adverse patterns and deliver remarkable, permanent change. Radically positive transformations are commonly observed in a patient's behavior within a four-week period.

Would I be asleep?

No, quite the opposite! Going back in time within the unconscious is achieved delving into an enhanced state of consciousness and provides vivid clarity of mind. Think of a form of '*hyper lucidity*' whilst in an '*in-between*' state, in which you gain direct access into *yourself* to look at facts with undisputable clarity.

Am I going to understand who I am?

We are whatever is left.

As we become aware of what pushes our buttons and pull our triggers, we can adopt a more vigilant approach towards our responsive behavior and trace back to the causal thoughts behind feelings. We can thus spot our adverse patterns, that will keep on manifesting until we have fully re-wired our thinking. Parting with your old, *conceptualised self* will invariably trigger an identity crisis for the ego that will go to war to resist change and vacuity.

How much money do you make doing this?

I must talk about money, the most frustrating aspect of my method; however improbable, I build a method that is too effective to make a living out of it! I rarely see a patient more than twice and word of mouth is anecdotal, with hypnosis still being heavily stigmatised. For the same reason, advertising works very little, if at all. And I regret to say that the very few hypnotherapists who became wealthy using the media have all exploited their patients, seeing them a lot more than they should. The job is that of a *mind plumber* (or *soul plumber* as a patient puts it); we unblock pipes of the mind and make way for the new to flow in. It's usually a one-off job. Who sees their plumber once a week for months?

With that in mind, part of your effort to rewire your mind is to train it (and your ego) to accept the notion that '*I am whatever is left*'. Once we have put down the armor, taken off the mask and shed each unnecessary layer, we are whatever is left. And what is left isn't the relevant part: once adverse patterns hurting us are broken, *we send the brain a signal of change towards the other direction*, to do things differently because the '*I*' is now thinking differently. *What's left* will be acting for your own good, which matters more than trying to attach a set of values and a sense of identification to it.

This deconstruction process of the ego often gives birth to a '*less is mo*re' environment which can be nurtured instead of always striving for *more*.

❧

MIND YOUR MIND

MIND YOUR MIND
18. ADVERSE PATTERNS AND THE ART OF ANGER

After looking at how old beliefs leading to false identification, we can now learn to defuse triggers behind adverse patterns affecting our daily business. These are sets of recurring thoughts acting against our emotional structure and triggered by stimuli systematically producing the same discomfort. Those stimuli are too many to identify to somehow expel from our system, but we can contain the impact they bear on a situation. This *stop and spot'* practice is done once we know to which belief a trigger is attached. Over time, it can become a second nature. First, we must distinguish two types of thought process, *functional* and *dysfunctional thinking*:

Functional Thinking (awareness and feedback):
- *my actions aren't fear driven, I act out of clarity*
- *I have aligned my actions with my wellbeing*
- thoughts are just thoughts*: I am not my thoughts*
- feelings are just feelings*: I am not my feelings*

Dysfunctional Thinking (*I am what I think*)
- feelings affect *my choices: I feel my decisions*
- I feed off *historic beliefs: I think what I believe*
- thoughts affect *my sense of self: I believe what I think*
- thoughts affect *my sense of self: I am my thoughts*
- *feelings affect my sense of self: I am my feelings*

At the risk of repeating myself to the Nth degree; Neither my feelings nor my thoughts are *who I am*, but if I let them, they can and will, shape my sense of identity.

Example of thoughts over self-perception:

Awareness: *I feel angry.*

Pause to reflect:

- *Can I revert to my thoughts just before I felt angry?*
- What *is the last thought I remember*?

  Thought identified:

  The last thing I remember is that lady walking past

  Can I identify the trigger?

- *Could the lady walking past make me feel angry?*
- *Why?*

I). **Trigger identified**:

she reminds me of an aunt who used to laugh at me when I was a child. It made me feel ashamed of myself. Seeing a stranger who reminds me (RE-MIND = RE-boot in my-MIND) of someone I know (*my aunt*) is making me feel angry right now.

Now that I paused and became aware of the thought triggering the feeling I can:

i) **step 1**: continue to observe the thought until I realise that the feeling attached to it has no value, and

ii) **step 2**: try to link it to one a core belief about myself I discovered in regression: in this example; *an aunt made me feel ashamed because I believed that being laughing material for someone is a shameful thing that made me feel terrible about myself.*

Because of who she looks like, someone triggers a past trauma, triggering anger to deal with repressed pain. If this flash self-analysis isn't enough, practice one of the tips described below in '*Stop Thinking*'.

II). **Trigger unidentified**: can't link a thought to this feeling of anger.

In that case trick your mind with a *dissociative process*, transferring your situation onto someone you love and care about. If that someone felt angry without knowing why, what would you say to them to quiet their mind? Write it down then read it '*from yourself to yourself*'. If that may sound like a weird thing, try it anyway, it even works on the most tenacious, stubborn souls.

Here is another example where you are very angry and this time, you do know why; you managed to identify your trigger. Say you are angry because you have been invited to a gala dinner, but you haven't been seated at the expected table where you think you belong with people of your social status. You tell yourself that the food will taste the same regardless of where you seat, you might meet lovely people at your table and even bond with some of them and yet, you are just mad with rage.

Awareness: I feel enraged.
Pause to reflect:
Why the rage?
- *I feel disrespected.*
- The hosts know me, and they should know better (oh look, another bunch who *should know better*).

Can I identify the trigger?
I can associate this situation to a similar event I revisited in regression. It happened at a theatre when I was eight. We were denied two of our seats because my dad couldn't afford to pay for all the tickets and was hoping to smuggle in his children for free. I sensed his embarrassment and felt shame for the first time. I

swore to myself that I would never have to put myself through such an ordeal ever again. And so, I did what was needed. I became a wealthy, respected member of society and upmarket clubs where I can be spotted at the best seats, always in the 'right' company. Here again, practicing the same exercise as before, to pause, observe, identify and let go of the thought should help get rid of the feeling, in this case, rage. When disturbed by feelings, a good second nature to develop is to think in terms of representations and ask yourself; *'can I link this event or individual to something or someone, for me to be feeling this way?'.* For instance, *'this friend reminds me of how fatalist and anxiogenic my grandmother used to be'.* You can now link that friend to the anxiety that your grandmother used to pass on to you. This helps defuse the feelings' intensity by contextualising their meaning. Conversely, you might want to dig and wonder if beyond the friendship is built on anything else than the familiarity of your grandmother, and whether it should be nurtured or gently parted with (remember *'shit stinks but it's warm'*).

Stop Thinking

Barring the brain from thinking will dissipate any feeling whatsoever. Not permanently, but here and now, to pull oneself together and refocus. These three, purely mechanical exercises always work when done properly.

I)   Asking yourself: *'I wonder what my next thought is going to be'.* This exquisitely simple idea authored by Eckhart Tolle brings one to realise that we are totally unable to know what we are going to think next. While going through the motions of this realisation we are no longer thinking of anything.

II) *Square* breathing (a.k.a. *'box breathing'*) was invented for and by *Navy Seals* to endure fear in combat situations. The idea behind it is to saturate our senses so that the act of thinking becomes impossible. And since without thinking we can't feel anything, my feeling fear, anxiety etc... goes away. Yes, it is that simple, and yes, it works.

The first time, use a square shape, such as a napkin, hold it to eye level, then, in that order;

i)   with your eyes, follow each of the square's four sides, *clockwise*

ii)   repeat i) this time counting from 1 to 4, for each side of the square, as you follow each side with your eyes (so; I count from 1 to 4, four times).

iii) repeat i) and ii) this time *breathing in* on side 1, *hold* your breath on side 2, *breathe out* on side 3 and *hold* on side 4.

iv) Repeat this exercise *'full square'* at least twice then answer the questions: *'what am I thinking'* and *'how am I feeling'*. The (mind blanking) result should puzzle your mind. You should find yourself thinking and feeling absolutely nothing.

Square breathing requires simultaneously using eye movement, to follow each side of the square and mind focus, to both count from one to four (for each side, as your eyes follow each of them) and pace your breathing across four periods of four seconds. It is the simultaneity of three tasks performed concurrently that leaves the brain unable to perform a fourth task, no matter what it is, including thinking. And no thinking: no feeling! No fear, no feeling inadequate, no anxiety, no panic. If it works for *Navy Seals* during combat, it should work when we are about to lose it behind the wheel on the road or if we are prone to panic attacks and get stuck in the Paris *metro*, the London *tube* or the New-York *subway*. The trick is to manage to think of square breathing (to *'square think'*) on time to neutralise that looming panic attack about to strike. For argument's sake, square breathing kills any feeling, therefore it also works if you wanted to stop being happy or stop laughing, just as it works to neutralise anxiety. Practicing square breathing should provide you evidence that despite being as complex as we think we are, the mind is easily saturated and is able to make room for the vacuity necessary to cleanse and regain self-control.

III)   This other exercise is like *square breathing* with a meditative twist: place a hand on your tummy. Raise your other hand and point the index finger upwards at eye level (much like an Indian divinity). Now gaze at the index finger, counting from one to eight. Then close your eyes, count from one to eight and this time, rub your stomach with each count. You should achieve a similar result of not being able to think at all.

I highly recommend practicing systematic, real-time thought *'search and destroy'* to identify and defuse your triggers. And in the process, remind yourself of these observations at will:
- feelings are produced by thoughts
- we are neither our thoughts nor our feelings
- thinking can be rewired

The Art of Anger
If you are angry, be angry. Celebrate your anger even, for it is the doorway to a more peaceful mind. Take a pen and paper and write down your anger; what and who you're angry at, and why. Let it all out. Knowing that no one will ever read that piece of

paper that you will burn later, write how far you'd go, retaliating against that person you are so angry with, if you must. Let that piece of paper be your mini *'rage journal'*. Go for it. When you are done, leave it there, walk out of the room, go outside, look at the sky and take a few, evenly paced, deep breaths. Then come back into the room, to the piece of paper. Read it. Don't skip a line. Notice how unreasonable and even extreme you might have been, but don't be alarmed by the tone or the words you used and don't engage in self-analysis. Instead, acknowledge where you have exaggerated and *what you could have said instead*. With a pen, *cross out the parts you'd like to remove* and *circle the parts you'd like to keep*. On a second piece of paper, using the circled parts from the first letter as a starting point, write what you could have said instead. Then *burn* the first letter and *watch it burn*. Leave the second, *latest* letter on the table, leave the room, go outside, look at the sky again, breathe evenly five times and come back into the room. Read the letter, circle what to keep and strike out what to remove. Take a third piece of paper, write down, again based on the circled parts of the second letter and add anything you feel guided to write. Then burn the second letter and watch it burn. Leave the room again. And *repeat the process until you are satisfied* with what the letter says. You may not have reached *'unconditional forgiving territory'* but your anger should have morphed into a more neutral sensation that should be palpable.

Dealing with anger first can spare one the agony of trying to jot down words of gratitude intended for someone we are mad with while the head feels like a pressure cooker on the verge of explosion. On the other hand, once the anger dissipates and reason regains the driving seat, it isn't uncommon to feel the act of forgiving within reach (when we *think* that we need to forgive someone) and even observe a growing compassion towards others that can result in greater inner peace.

Allow me a brief mention of co-dependency. It is essentially, both a behavioural pathology and an addiction leading one to do two things; 1) switch around the *avoidant*, the *people pleaser* or the *abuser* types and 2) build unreasonable -*and* unspoken- expectations inevitably leading to prolonged resentment and near constant anger. Notably, this imbalanced emotional and mental structure forces many to act out with systematic kindness. It isn't a choice. So, my message is; if you come across such individuals, never take their kindness for granted and try to gently direct them to "*Codependent No More*" the lifesaving bible on the topic by Melodie Beattie.

෨

MIND YOUR MIND
19. OUR REAL BLESSINGS AND MEDITATION

Positive thinking never worked on me. But if I start off with unbundling my negative thinking and walk back following a deconstruction process, I end up achieving a state of neutrality or even positivity. Likewise, counting my blessings works best if I start with counting the plagues not affecting me and gratitude towards others only works once I have got rid of any negativity that I feel towards them.

Blessings We Don't Pay Attention To

Can the absence of discomfort and displeasures that could be affecting us be counted as a blessing? A blessing in disguise is often referred to as a situation we could have engaged in but that somehow became out of reach and which, in hindsight, spared us pain and unpleasantness. But there are also hundreds of drawbacks not affecting us and that we don't count as blessings, outside the occasional thought, usually triggered by hearing about the suffering of others in the media or from friends or family. If you are healthy, I urge you to recognise that as a daily blessing, write it down or say it out loud each morning and every night for at least a week. I put together a few mantras that can ease everyday interaction between our narcissistic self and another eight billion narcissistic selves:

- *'Billions of individuals live in unconscious fear'.*
- *'Trying to guess what others think of me is a lost cause; even if I were to ask, they would probably not tell me the truth'.*
- *'Guessing what others think of me is only a waste of energy and mind power'.*

- *'If people look at me it doesn't mean they think anything of me'* (if they do, why does it matter?).
- *'People not noticing me is usually not the result of a conscious effort to not notice me'* (and if it was, why does it matter?).
- *'I never walk with my head down'* (chin up!)
- *'No-one is my enemy. No-one is my friend. Everyone is my teacher'*.

I also listed basic wellbeing lifestyle tips to try for a week. Whilst I have undoubtedly stated the obvious for lots of you, practicing these simple steps isn't necessarily easy for others. Hopefully, it will help some to focus and regain control.

- Sleep in a screen-free room. If your phone is your alarm clock, then switch it on airplane mode until the next morning.
- Listen to music you find grounding. The mind can be conditioned greatly with music. Do not stop at so called healing music but try different kinds until you find frequencies that resonate, help you focus, stay still, feel calmer and sleep.
- Eat a diet of greens, fruit, lots of water, ban junk food and sugar drinks like the plague.

With healthy tips, it is often a case of '*whatever works*' and with practice you should find yourself going back and forth with some of those tips and of course, you should use your imagination and appetite to explore ideas that may work to your advantage, to create your own routine.

And with that, onto our last, but not least, topic which I purposely kept for the end because of its importance: the power of setting intentions and the virtues of prayer. Religious and *God*less.

MIND YOUR MIND
20. THE POWER OF INTENTION AND PRAYER

You obviously don't need to be religious to be spiritual or to pray. *God*less prayers are still prayers.

One can even argue that the dogma-free agnostic without bias towards any form of spirituality (religious or non-religious) might be more spiritually elevated than a believer locked into a specific faith (in most cases, not chosen but imposed as a matter of birth circumstances). Irrespective of any faith, the act of praying comes with great physiological benefits that can positively influence your day and your sleep. Therefore, praying is probably a good idea and doing so in the morning and in the evening probably the best time to do it. You can pray to almost anything that resonates within, not just for your football team to win. As a guideline, the prayers below rank among the most popular ones, based on obligations and personal circumstances:

- Adoration: praising *God*
- Contrition: asking for *God*'s forgiveness.
- Communion: all day any time
- Contemplative: meditative
- Festive prayers: *Easter*, *Thanksgiving* etc...
- Intercession: on behalf of others
- Petition: asking *God* for a favour.
- Prayers of agreement: corporate prayer
- Repetition: ask for the same favour repeatedly
- Spiritual warfare: with yourself, Satan, or demons
- Supplication: lift your needs
- Watch and pray: continual conscious praying

Persistent prayer can also be thought of as a type of repetitive prayer, good for requests that we've had or prayed about for years: the healing of a loved one, of a broken relationship or the forgiveness of a habitual sin. I find this type of prayer fitting particularly well into the '*healthy mind conditioning*' kind we saw earlier that contributes to cleansing the brain, as opposed to the '*unhealthy brainwashing*' spurting out of our phones (except for the odd zen meditation *app*).

I would encourage you to look for what resonates, to listen to various prayers but also and especially, listen to your inner self, your imagination, write up your own mantras and your own prayer. Also, listen to prayers in other languages, particularly *Aramaic*, which is said to have the highest spiritual vibration and which in my opinion, sounds incredibly uplifting. If you are up for it, memorise and repeat prayers in a language like *Aramaic*, which, like an '*OM*' or a *Sufi* chant should make you feel lighter, more serene and more elevated. In terms of posture, it is important to find one that feels right, as long as you are able to breathe properly (which is as important as posture). However, I recommend getting on your knees at least once. You might find it strange at first, but it can be followed with a sense of relief which you might find enjoyable and wish to repeat. It is part of experiencing humility. Humility is not humiliation. If you feel *humiliated* on your knees it means that mental projections beamed by your ego are succumbing to distress and panic as you do something too far outside your *comfort zone*. Just '*hit the knees*' at least once.

Because of the complete absence of negative side effects, any downside or financial cost, I would urge anyone who doesn't pray to give it a try. Especially If you are a ferocious atheist!

A survey carried out by *Johns Hopkins Medicine* over four thousand individuals who experienced '*ultimate reality*' or '*God*' has shown that it confers lasting benefits to mental health. The experiences, whether spontaneous or originated by a psychedelic, resulted in a similar positive impact. Among those who reported experiencing personal encounters with *God*, researchers found that more than two-thirds of self-identified atheists subsequently shed that label, regardless of whether the encounter was organic or induced by psychedelics. These results, favouring the benefits of meditation and altered states of consciousness (such as *guided regression* by the way) are however biased when it comes to the relation with a *God*. Let's not forget that, were it not for the *God* mythology being ingrained in our minds since childhood, whether one believes in a *God* or not, we are all deeply brainwashed to link intense feelings of lucidity and clarity of mind to a divine connection. In other words, if the God story had never been branded into humanity's collective psyche, who knows how those experiences would be worded instead...

The most powerful (and arguably, the ultimate narcissistic trip) force I experienced is faith in myself as a result of intentions I set but not intentions I bashed my head to believe in. I am referring to high conviction intentions that felt like they reflect what's right for me deep-down. A great and simple way to set intentions is to test their authenticity with setting meaningless intentions at first ('*I am flying to the moon next week*', '*I will be able to learn a new language per day*') and gradually move towards more refined, realistic intentions ('*I can live with less, wealth is elsewhere*', '*I don't have to endure this or that*'). Then meditate over the best intention for you to set, right now. To do that, you can just close your eyes, focus on breathing slower, count from one to ten, rubbing your tummy with each breath and your forehead clockwise. Then focus on the phrase '*the best intention for me right now is* and fill in the blank with what comes to mind. If the answer is '*to make me a sandwich*'; try again. If this feels like another *wishy-washy* trick, I still urge you to give it a try before forming an opinion about something that only your ego is overseeing and vetting right now.

A French quote came to mind: 'only idiots don't change their mind'. I would instead use a belief I hold on to (and that is dangerously very close to becoming a *conviction*): *only* the *higher self can change the mind.*

With that, I can only wish for this book to help one find their way to their *original, higher self* and set in motion one of Rumi's quietly powerful quotes: '*every mortal will taste death but only some will taste life*'.

྾

THE END

21. SUMMARY

Here are the book's key take-home points to the instant-gratification addicts who couldn't possibly envision reading a book from start to finish and jumped from the '*Introduction*' section straight here:

- *We are not aware of why we do what we do.*
- *Our subconscious runs the show behind our back.*
- *We aren't our thoughts, yet we let them shape us.*
- *Rewiring how we think can change <u>and</u> save lives.*

A word on where we might be heading

Today, no one cares about magnets. besides fridge stickers, we have a vague idea of their use and are largely unimpressed by them. But four hundred years ago, if you sat in a tavern, moved a magnet under your table to make a coin *magically* move over its surface, you would have been tried for witchcraft. If in 2000 you stated that mobile phones would become *smart*, be barely used for calls but run our lives through the web, geo-localisation and A.I, few would have believed it. No matter how exponentially fast technology rockets, our imagination keeps failing us when projecting into the future. Especially one with us in it. It's okay to predict '*crazy stuff*' within two hundred and fifty years once we'll all be gone (will we though?) but don't you dare say that thirty years from now, capitalism will have imploded, lockdowns will be normalised and face to face interactions avoided by most. Here is by the by, a classic case of *cognitive dissonance* at work; the change-averse ego, shielding the mind from *unknown unknown* reaching for the nearest *comfort zone* where we feed our denial feeds with *confirmation bias*, sourced effortlessly online. Dismissing whistle blowers as fear-mongering catastrophists and cancelling anyone who threatens our mental architecture has never been easier. To hell with who foresaw the potential of smart phones twenty years ago, or the devastating damage of climate change fifty years ago. That is not to say that well-worded prophetic flair should be embraced as gospel, but systematic old school rebuttals to refuse new paradigms that are already taking us to truly bewildering unchartered territories, is keeping us asleep behind the wheel (*comfort zone* etc...).

Mindfulness is the least we can do, to cope with constant adaptation trough dwindling cycles, virtual interactions fostering poorer human proximity and *bioengineering* propaganda. China voting in favour of *augmented children* isn't giving the rest of the world much of a choice, if we don't want to be left behind by legions of next *gen* super-children powered with IQs averaging one hundred and thirty. It means that in the future, the likes of six-year-old *YouTube* sensation Mikail Akar, contemporary artist child prodigy, whose paintings sell for five thousand Euros a pop, will be normalised and go largely unnoticed. Recent quantum leaps in neurology, *A.I* and *V.R* could usher in a future where, just as science fiction is becoming the new science, virtual reality could supplant reality. We might end up couched, wired up into *V.R* hubs neuro feeding us such tailored sophisticated hedonism that we'll gradually ditch the '*real thing*' in favour of the '*simulated thing*', too perfectly adjusted to our current mood and heartbeat, 24/7. Imagine telepathically flicking through a holographic menu to pick safer, more enjoyable experiences than trying a new diner, holiday destination, meet up, socialise, date or have sex. Here again, don't let your imagination bridle your projecting into the future and consider that, just as my generation can feel nostalgic about writing and receiving letters, two hundred years from now, we might telepathically commiserate, about how we miss...speaking...

Are there benefits beyond the horror of it all?

Think, healthcare, climate and criminality. The benefits are likely to be so overwhelming, they'll be demanded by most and favour the demonisation of the opposition. Think how unpopular *you* would be to oppose, longer lives, better -free- healthcare, lower virus contagion due to the disappearance of physical money, and zero criminality? All that because you didn't want to be chipped. Think of a new regime, massaged into the collective psyche for its health, social, geopolitical and environmental benefits; nine billion souls no longer eating meat, flying nor driving would reduce Co^2 emissions to levels that would justify the titanic amounts of energy and resources it required to create it. Even more so if human breathing is substituted by electrical power! As megalopolis become more populated, what better way to decongest traffic and prevent civil conflicts or wars than by keeping everyone *blissfully anesthetised* at home? Rewarding citizens staying in, penalising those going beyond their monthly outdoor allowance. I can think of three, "*low hanging fruits*" major benefits derived from super A.I and bioengineering.

World hunger, could be defeated not through biodiversity and genetically modified abundance but with, *literally suppressing hunger*, alongside...the entire human digestive system. Imagine our great great-grand-children, browsing virtual *museums* streaming scenes of agriculture, people eating food and *toilet seat relics*. During and after such transition, the gourmets of this world won't suffer *food porn nostalgia* since the brain's reward system will be satisfied on-demand with customised neuro-digital re-creations of the finest *côte de boeuf* you have ever had, washed down with a *St Emilion* which will blow your mind away every time. What's not to like?

Healthcare and zero criminality.

Imagine health monitored 24/7 and preventive medicine finally becoming the dominant practice after the pharma lobbies were defeated by the reshuffling of capitalism. In exchange for a cheap or free chip implant we will access superior mental health and well-being during longer lives experienced a lot less pain and no more depression and anxiety. As for crimes, well, at first, as in *Minority Report*, criminals will be arrested before committing the crime they were about to commit but, as predictive tech improves, criminal impulses will probably be neutralised altogether. This means that, from running a traffic light to committing the worst atrocity such as molesting a child, breaking rules won't need to be punished anymore; it'll be gone before it happens. Imagine how incredibly popular such outcomes would be: fabulous health, longer lives and near zero criminality.

Last but not least; organised religion...

Let's be honest here; besides tainted spirituality, what do organised Abrahamic religions provide? Tribes, folklore, existential gap fillers, an invisible Godly ear to share or ask anything. God is *the answer when there is no answer*, albeit not delivering any. Imagine for a second, an omniscient, omnipresent, omnipotent *A.I.* life partner, diagnosing your child's complications before they emerge. Compare that to unanswered prayers to God to save your child who was diagnosed too late and dies as a result. Which *God* would you rather follow? One who consistently ignores your prayers or one that looks after you so reliably well that it even prevents disasters to happen in the first place? The downside might be that super A.I might make us feel like Gods ourselves, or worship it as the new God, but let's assume (dare I say "*pray*") that it will be smart enough to also ensure that we don't fall into that trap. I thus believe that A.I is set to replace or eradicate organised religion and open the door to a dogma-free spirituality.

At that point, freewill will have been traded out, with or without our consent, for continuous instant gratification of the highest grade. And chances are that by that time, we won't care. Until such a dystopian world pans out, your mind is our greatest ally but also the most coveted hackable commodity. Taking care of your mind is more critical than ever and to that effect, please find a short '*how to*' survival guide on the following and last page.

❧

22. SURVIVAL GUIDE.

Without
- Watch out for *brainwashing machines*
- If you are enrolled in a *cult, get out of it*
- Strive to avoid and flee *indoctrination*
- Strive to *live by example* and be your own leader
- When you're wrong, *admit* it, to your *self*
- Don't chase happiness but pursue *fulfilment*
- *Keep away* from what brings upset
- Think of *adaptability* as a key to stability
- Engage in situations challenging your *resilience*

Wellness
- Don't sleep with *YouTube* on
- Look for music that forges mental *equilibrium*
- Practice regular outdoor *physical activities*
- Eat a *soulful diet*, try vegetarianism or veganism
- Remember to *breathe* well and to be present
- Practice *sun gazing* during sunrise and sunset
- Learn to stop thinking; '*square breathe*' it
- Be *grateful* for burdens not affecting you
- Stay *physically connected* to people you love

Within
- *Identify* your beliefs and anchorage stands
- *Observe* the thoughts behinds your feelings
- Don't identify with thoughts or feelings
- You often already are what you admire in others
- Write about your negativity till it dissipates
- Pray *God*'s way or your way
- *Aim not for a shame-free life*
- Make your ego your *amigo*...

ABOUT THE AUTHOR

After two decades wandering in the London corporate world, frustrated and overpaid, Axel became an underpaid regression hypnotherapist and an improbable writer, striving to vulgarise opaque topics, occasionally with a tad of humour. Leading patients achieve major breakthroughs inspired him to share his experience and findings with a wider audience through this book.